FROM ROBBINS TO RIO

FROM ROBBINS TO RIO

A Miracle Journey

CELESTER AND CYNTHIA NEELEY

Scriptures unmarked or marked KJV are from the KING JAMES VERSION (KJV):
KING JAMES VERSION, public domain, unless otherwise noted.
NKJV: Scripture taken from the NEW KING JAMES VERSION®. Copyright© 1982
by Thomas Nelson, Inc. Used by permission. All rights reserved.
NIV: taken from THE HOLY BIBLE, NEW INTERNATIONAL VERSION®, NIV®
Copyright © 1973, 1978, 1984, 2011 by Biblica, Inc.® Used by permission.
All rights reserved worldwide.
AMP: taken from the Amplified® Bible (AMP), Copyright © 2015
by The Lockman Foundation. Used by permission. lockman.org
KJ21: Scripture quotations taken from the 21st Century King James Version®,
copyright © 1994. Used by permission of Deuel Enterprises, Inc., Gary, SD 57237.
All rights reserved.

Front cover art by Mark Rouse
©2023 Mark Rouse/mark@markrouse.com

Cover Design
Kayla Kennada/kayla4god@hotmail.com

Publisher, Editor, Interior Design, and Layout
Mary Jo Rennert Gremling/Bestwine Press/maryjo@bestwinepress.com

ISBN: 978-0-9899888-8-9

PRINTED IN THE UNITED STATES OF AMERICA
10 9 8 7 6 5 4 3 2 1

I would like to dedicate this book to our Creator, almighty God, for calling me out of darkness to His Son Jesus. Also, to my wife and partner, Cynthia, and our three beautiful daughters, Cyndee, Paula, and Dara. They listened and heard and chose to follow the direction of the Holy Spirit to become strong women of God. And to our three grandchildren, Michael, Mekel, and Phillip.

1

Our Journey Begins

I was awakened by the jetliner's speaker system as the overhead lights came on to indicate that breakfast was being served. "We will be landing in forty-five minutes," came the announcement as the flight attendant asked us if we wanted coffee or juice. I ordered coffee for my wife and me, and our two daughters chose juice as they stretched themselves awake. I could feel that something new and different was happening in our lives that December 26, 1984, without understanding exactly what it was.

After landing in Brazil an hour later, we passed through the passport and baggage check and into a new world that was crowded and hot. Most of the people spoke the native language, Portuguese. We met with our host, who separated us into two vehicles for our trip to Seropedica, our new home for the next year. An hour later, we arrived in a town about forty miles south of Rio de Janeiro. It was a rural, grassy place with no traffic lights. Most people were walking or riding bicycles.

We soon reached the home base of Mission Volantes de Cristo. Our work was to study how they conducted rural missions in planting new churches and evangelizing cities and towns in the interior states of Brazil. Our team consisted of my wife Cynthia, our two youngest daughters (Paula, 16, and Dara, 14) and me. Our daughter Cynthia was in Indiana attending Ball State University.

Rio de Janeiro is about 5,000 miles from Anderson, Indiana, where we are from. Living in Brazil was a dream come true for me—so different from my birthplace, Robbins, Illinois, a small town south of Chicago, where I grew up with my two sisters, our parents, both sets

Living in Brazil was a dream come true for me.

of grandparents, uncles, aunts, and cousins. We moved into the city of Chicago when I was eleven, then to Calumet Park after the death of our mother.

I was a dreamer, and I had always dreamed of leaving Robbins, Blue Island, Calumet Park, and the South Side of Chicago for anywhere else. Brazil was not a place I had dreamed of, but it was where I moved our family in 1984.

How we became involved with this mission

It all began after I accepted Christ as my Savior. My wife and I began thinking and talking about how we could give back for what the Lord had done for us in our business. We owned our own music and novelty stores at that time, which were expanding, and after a trip to the Caribbean, we could see there was a chance for our kind of business in other locations. We dreamed of opening a store or stores in the Caribbean islands.

As we continued to grow in our faith, we opened our home to provide for a Brazilian mission leader while he was speaking at our church. He was seeking help for his mission work in Brazil, and we learned a few words and a little about his country. After a

2

short-term visit to Brazil, we knew the Lord was calling us to that nation. Our hearts and faith began to reach out for what the Lord wanted us to do, and it became clear to us that we were to answer a call that was in our hearts to work in Brazil. Many negative things were happening in our lives and our church that almost destroyed our ability to continue our journey.

The Word of God had shown us that the gifts and calling of the Lord for us were right, and what the Lord had given us was for us. The Holy Spirit is faithful, and the right doors began to open for us to serve in Brazil. We knew that our prayers and plans were in the hands of the Lord, and our excitement continued to grow. The Lord is seeking workers to come into His harvest. The anointing of evangelism was upon us.

How we overcame the financial challenge

The financial provision we received was a miracle. We needed to cover the cost of round-trip tickets for a family of four and the money necessary to support us for six months. Our church (Good News) was a big help with this. I remember the day when a member of our church stopped by our home to talk with me about how the financial part of our plans was going. He began to tell me what had happened to him that morning on the way to work. That was the reason for his visit. He asked me how everything was going for our trip, which was coming up in a few weeks. I told him we were not where we needed to be financially but we were trusting the Lord. He said that the Spirit told him to give me all the money he had been saving for a few house repairs in his home. He reached in his pocket and pulled out a wad of cash and handed me a gift of more than a thousand dollars. He said, "This will help with your trip." I was stunned and overjoyed for this gift and saw how the Creator of the universe can supply our needs when we ask, pray, and believe—that nothing is impossible.

After making all the necessary arrangements for our eldest daughter, who was enrolled in the University, we were able to finalize our travel plans. We headed south to Miami for our plane trip to Rio de Janeiro.

While we were on the flight to Brazil, I had the opportunity to think about all the things that had happened to us before we departed for this trip. There was another member from our church who had asked us to drive a vehicle to Miami, our point of departure, and deliver it to his brother. During our trip, the vehicle developed a mechanical problem that could have destroyed all our plans. After we found a repair shop, the mechanic informed us that the vehicle needed a part, but he probably couldn't get it in time because it was just two days before Christmas. Cynthia and I joined hands and prayed, and shortly afterward the mechanic told us he had found what he needed and could have our van ready to roll in two hours. We were laughing and crying over this answer to our prayers.

We arrived in Miami and caught our flight to Rio on December 25, 1984, arriving the next morning at a hot humid airport for this adventure with the Lord.

A place for our family
We stayed in the home of our host for the first two weeks before we rented a house not far from the Mission where we needed to be. That house was not a permanent solution, but it served us well: a living room, two bedrooms, a kitchen area, and a toilet. When it rained, the roof leaked, and cute little frogs with suction-cup feet came in through every opening into the house and

climbed onto the toilet, sink, face bowl, and fridge. On rainy nights, the girls would scream out for fear of the frogs with big glassy eyes. We suffered one break-in while we lived there, and we were relieved when a short time later, we rented a larger, more secure place that would be our home.

Finding a school

Our hosts had located three schools that taught in English for our daughters, so we arranged to visit those schools. The first one was our choice, but it was the most expensive of the three. We met with the headmaster and explained that we were working with the Mission, representing our church, helping the Mission update some of their teachings and applications of the Word of God.

We knew this was a gift from heaven. It was the same school where all the multinational companies and consulate workers sent their children.

He invited us to enroll our daughters and explained the cost of attending the Escola Americana do Rio de Janeiro. I explained to him that we were missionaries, and our church could not pay the amount they were asking. I inquired if they had any scholarships available.

We talked a little more, and I explained that our girls were good students and more than deserving to go to a good school. He thought for a few minutes then said, "Mr. Neeley, enroll your daughters in our school, and let's see what happens." We did, and we knew this was a gift from heaven. It was the same school where all the multinational companies and consulate workers sent their children. It had to be good even with a slogan on the wall that said "Humanism."

For the first week of school, I rode the buses with my daughters, showing them the terminals they should use, the buses they should catch, what and whom to watch out for, and what to do. The trip took two hours each way in good weather and nearly three on bad days.

Our key to success

Prayer was our key to success, along with reading and studying the Word of God and confessing those promises that were revealed to us. We were about five thousand miles from Anderson, our home city, and the only sure thing we had was the Word of God. Doors began to open for us and opportunities became available as we stumbled every step of the way and lifted our voices to the Lord in prayer.

Our daughters attended the best school in the city of Rio. Cynthia and I had a limited vocabulary in Portuguese, so our girls became our interpreters for that first season of our mission work.

Our first assignment with the Mission was to evangelize at a rock music festival called Rock-n-Rio.

Our first assignment with the Mission was to evangelize at a rock music festival called Rock-n-Rio, which attracted some of the top rock music artists from around the world. Our job was to hand out Christian flyers, speak English to English-speaking visitors, and explain to them there was a better way for their lives. We passed out flyers printed in Portuguese, Spanish, and English to attendees and asked questions about why they were at this event. The crowds were huge and hungry for something new. We did not know this at the time, but the presence of the Spirit of God was strong there. This was a good introduction to street evangelism Brazilian-style for us.

The American School

Our two teenagers adjusted to this new country, language, culture, and climate and made friends a lot faster than we did. It was the Lord working in their hearts. We remembered their response when we first told them about our plans to move to Brazil. They did not want to go. But now they were adapting to our new environment—talking and laughing, living without TV, McDonalds, computers, and all the amenities they were used to in Anderson.

Our main concern was the bus trip from our town to the other side of the city of Rio, which could have been dangerous without the Lord's help. The school was located on the back side of a huge mountain that was the largest poor neighborhood in Rio. Armed guards were stationed every day and all day to watch over the place. There were never any problems that we knew of at the school, but there were a few attempted thefts on the bus ride to and from.

Understanding divine grace helped us have the peace we needed. On one of their bus trips back home from school, the bus driver pulled over to the side of the road and all the passengers started getting off and standing outside the bus, so our girls joined them.

The driver explained to them that the electrical system for the outside lights was not working. He was not going to remain on the side of the road but would continue to Seropedica, the final stop. In the area where this happened, there were not any streetlights or outside lights of any kind.

The driver told everyone that the trip would be dangerous and all who wanted to continue could get back on the bus. Those who wanted to wait for the next bus could wait for its arrival. A few passengers and our girls got back on the bus with no outside lights and began the balance of their trip to our town without outside lights.

The girls said people were laughing and talking, and every time they went around a curve or over a bridge, the others would shout, "Oba, Oba!" Our daughters told us we would have thought the passengers were at a soccer game cheering for goals. They arrived safely in Seropedica, laughing and talking as if nothing had happened. Our girls knew that we were praying daily for their safety, but this account was a little unsettling. The Mission had given us a car for the short trip to the last bus stop, so we waited for them there. That day, when they got in the car, the girls began to tell us this unbelievable story. Once again, we thanked the Lord that His promises were real: "I will never leave you or forsake you." We asked them lots of questions, especially about what the bus driver said. They told us he spoke street Portuguese, which was filled with lots of slang. The ride did not seem dangerous to our daughters. They appeared to be adapting to their daily journey to the city and making new friends.

2

The Road to Brazil

I grew up in a small midwestern town south of Chicago, Illinois, the son of parents and grandparents raised in the South. My two sisters and I were taught at an early age the basics of working hard, obedience, church, and doing good (or else we felt the sting of a switch or a belt). We were poor among the poor, but we did not know it because we had adults in our lives who loved us and did the best they could to guide us in the right way. In the atmosphere we lived in, we heard, saw, and experienced two paths. Christianity and obeying the Bible and the leaders of the church were one path. The other path was the world and the bad and not-so-bad in a small town: drinking, cussing, prostitution, unmarried or abandoned families, gambling, knife fights, thievery, and the like.

After I attended grade school, our family moved into the city, which was what most of my friends wanted to do. Following high school and marriage and attending college night classes, I was hired to work for an airline for a season.

When our third daughter was born, we decided to move out of Chicago, to raise our children according to different rules. We made our way to Anderson, Indiana, where we opened a music store that grew into four stores in Anderson and Indianapolis.

When we moved from Chicago and started a business in Anderson, Indiana, we never imagined that business would lead us to missionary work in Brazil. We had dreams of owning a music store after I had managed one in Chicago. That first store grew into a larger store, and after three years, we added novelties and opened a second store in Indianapolis. That store also grew, so we added a third and fourth store, which also did well.

The battle in my mind

I was searching for something, but I did not know what it was until my wife had a serious surgery and she started to read the Bible. After the operation, she started going to Bible study regularly and growing in a way I could not understand, but I knew it was good. She guided our girls into the church and Sunday school as I was working hard to grow our business. I would take them to Bible study and watch sports programs on the pastor's TV. I was not interested in this small storefront church.

My wife told me that the pastor was having problems with his car and asked me to look at it, which I did. While checking out the car, I heard a voice speaking on the inside of me say, "Fix it." It was not a suggestion but a command: "Fix it." I had the money and time, so I gave his car a tune-up and took it to the place where the pastor was living, handed the keys to him, and told him it was working fine now. After that event and a few others, I could not go back to what I used to be.

My goal at that time was to become a millionaire. As we expanded distribution to Kentucky and Illinois, I began to experience problems with stress and confusion and looked for help. I knew there was a God who created all things, so I turned my attention to heaven and accepted Jesus as my Lord and Savior and gave my heart to Him, and things began to change. I was filled with the Holy Spirit, spoke that heavenly language, and began having visions, dreams, and revelations. God was now real to me. By His Spirit, He began to guide my footsteps, relationships, thoughts, desires, and attitude.

For the first time in my life, I could discern the Lord talking to me about me, and I heard Him say if I continued on this road, my life would come to an end. I was still young and was not interested in hearing about death, so, in my prayers, I asked the Lord, "What should I do?"

"Let go of this idol and turn your life over to me."

It was the most difficult decision I have ever made, but I did it and watched all my dreams go down the drain. We went through a painful bankruptcy that opened my eyes to what it means to be called by the Lord. I, my wife, and my family had a calling on our lives that I did not understand. We lost everything—even our home—and when I hit the bottom, I said to the Lord, "Now what?" I heard the Lord say, "I will rebuild your life on faith in Me."

After that word, nothing else mattered. The Lord was in control. I tried to explain to the Lord that I had responsibilities to my wife and three girls. I needed to put food on the table and gas in the car. I had bills to pay. By the grace of the Lord, we continued to live in our house for another year debt-free. As I think back to that period, I'm amazed at how I thought I was informing the Lord about something He already knew—He knows everything!

I found a job managing a fast-food location while I studied the Bible day and night. I saw my new life in Christ begin to grow as the Lord helped us rebuild our life on faith in Christ alone. Doors began to open for us as we helped everyone who needed help. There were not many churches in Anderson with active foreign missionaries, and we could feel the tug of the Spirit to go beyond our city and state. We expanded our ministry to other cities in Indiana, Illinois, Ohio, and Kentucky and satisfied that call to foreign missions by going to the Caribbean Islands, Haiti, Puerto Rico, the Dominican Republic, and the islands of the Bahamas. The only prayer we could pray was "Thank You, Lord, for all You have done for us."

Our road to Brazil began after the pastor of our church returned from a mission trip to Latin America. In a Sunday morning service after his return, he told us about the many things the Lord had

The only prayer we could pray was "Thank You, Lord, for all You have done for us."

done for them in the places they went to and how they were moved to commit our church to help where we could. One of these places was Brazil.

After the service, we talked with the pastor and listened to how we might help. He explained to us about a Brazilian mission that needed help with the work they were doing. They offered to do an exchange with us, send some of our people to help them, and let them send a few of their members to work with us in the United States. As he was explaining the plan, the first names that came to his mind were ours, and he asked if we would pray and seek direction from the Lord about going to represent our church. We did, and, in the process, we received three verbal confirmations that we were to go. We had never received such an invitation like this before, so we asked the Lord, and He confirmed that we should do this. We took up the challenge, and three members—my wife, another female, and I—went from our church to Brazil for a successful three-month trial.

After our return, our church went through a split, and we put our plan for a return trip on the shelf and forgot about Brazil as we worked to repair the damage from the split. A new church was born called Good News, and we helped set up the new church as we continued to communicate with the Brazilian mission.

3

Our Early Days With the Mission

After we became familiar with Seropedica and the other small cities nearby, our next challenges were to learn the language, get to know the culture, and adapt to the food. We felt as if we were climbing a mountain blindfolded with our hands tied.

Foreign mission work is dangerous when you do not know the language, the culture, and the food. Those are the big three giants in the land. Without a growing understanding of what someone is saying, ignorance can destroy whatever it is you are trying to do. We worked overtime on all of these during our first year in Brazil. The most difficult for us was language.

How could I help the mission?

I began to fix the things in the Mission that needed repair, and with only a very few tools and little money, the Spirit of God began to open doors for us to obtain everything we needed. We learned that if we did the things we could do, the Lord would make a way for the things we could not do. Our job was to learn and help where we could. We were in Brazil to help the mission, which had trouble with finances, vehicles, attracting new students, and transportation. My mechanical and electrical background had prepared me for this, so I enjoyed helping to get everything working as it should, when language was not necessary.

Cynthia and I began to receive invitations to speak at a few Bible studies and local churches near the school, and word began to circulate that the Mission had Americans working with them and that the Mission was doing something different. We did not know what this meant to the school or to us. We could see that something was happening as the Word of God came to life in the city.

We saw the Word of the Lord in the Gospel of Mark come alive to us: *"Go into all the world and preach the gospel to every creature. He who believes and is baptized will be saved; but he who does not believe will be condemned. And these signs will follow those who believe: In My name they will cast out demons; they will speak with new tongues; they will take up serpents; and if they drink anything deadly, it will by no means hurt them; they will lay hands on the sick, and they will recover." ... And they went out and preached everywhere, the Lord working with them and confirming the word through the accompanying signs* (Mark 16:15-18, 20 NKJV).

No matter what the problem was, we prayed for God's solution and not the problem.

The Spirit taught us how to pray for the needs of the people we came in contact with in every church and Bible study. No matter what the problem was, we prayed for God's solution and not the problem.

The Mission was a training school for missionaries. The courses included English, basic Bible, evangelism, Portuguese, prayer, and discipleship. This door gave us freedom to show them how to pray for the sick, cast out demons, and enter into spiritual warfare. Other traditional mission schools did not include teaching about warfare and the power of the Holy Spirit gifts and fruit of the Spirit.

A new way to celebrate Carnival

We learned to adapt ourselves to their national sport, football (which we know as soccer), and Carnival celebration in Rio, which helped us understand Brazilian culture. We were invited to attend a Christian retreat away from the city during Carnival time. Most of the churches in the city did retreats during Carnival time, abandoning the city to parades, parties, and orgies for four days.

I heard Him say, "Tell these people that retreats during Carnival time is not My will for them."

The leaders asked me to speak at one of the teaching sessions to encourage the churches. As I was preparing a message and listening to the Lord, I heard Him say, "Tell these people that retreats during Carnival time is not My will for them."

I said, "Lord that's what this is. I was invited to encourage the church during this time."

"I want you to tell them to hear this word which I am giving you."

In obedience, I told the people at the retreat what God had said. I began by introducing my wife and told them how we were honored to be with them. When I repeated what the Lord had said to me about this meeting, I was not sure my interpreter would tell

17

them what the Lord had told me. I felt a hush sweep through the room as I saw the surprise on the faces of everyone.

"Did I not say in My Word that My people are the light of the world, and they should let their light shine so the world can see and glorify My Father? When all the believers leave the city, you leave it in darkness, and the force of darkness rules the city. Have your church retreat in your own buildings, in your own neighborhoods, with the lights on and the doors open, singing praise songs, and see what I will do."

The anointing of the Lord began to touch hearts, and tears began to flow as I continued to call for prayer and praise for the city of Rio de Janeiro, calling on the Lord for mercy for those trapped in darkness. That word was not received by everyone, but it certainly woke up those who were listening. The following year, a few of the churches did what the Spirit directed and had their Carnival celebration in their neighborhood churches. They gave testimony of how many people from the streets came in and how many people gave their hearts to Jesus. Revival came to churches both large and small as the power of the Holy Spirit visited during Carnival time. In the years that followed, it spread to other cities and churches. When the church lifts the name of Jesus and glorifies our heavenly Father, good things happen—even during Carnival.

Why Brazil?
We have been asked this question: "Why did you choose Brazil to do mission work? There are plenty of places here in the US that need help and have people who need to hear what you are saying." The calling of the Lord did not make sense to us. We did not have the background or education for what we were doing. We knew this calling from the Lord was different. It resonated in our hearts

that this was the Lord. We did not choose to work in Brazil. We were looking for a way to give back for all the blessings that had come to us. In the Caribbean, nothing seemed to resonate for us. The doorway to Brazil opened for us by invitation from a Brazilian missionary who visited our church seeking help with what they were trying to do in their country. After our pastor returned from a trip to Brazil, he asked for volunteers to go to Brazil and help.

We volunteered to go on a short-term mission trip to see what we could do, and after a lot of prayer, Cynthia and I plus one other female agreed to serve for three months. We arrived and worked alongside Brazilian Christian missionaries in the training school and various works they had founded.

On our return trip to Anderson, I could not sleep because I was thinking about our experience with the Mission. I asked the Lord in prayer if we could return to the Mission again later. The Lord challenged me to get rid of everything that would stop or slow us down and to prepare ourselves for returning

On our return trip to Anderson, I could not sleep because I was thinking about our experience with the Mission.

to Brazil. When I shared this with my wife, she asked the question, "What about my piano?" I responded that was the first thing on my list.

We prayed, asking the Lord many questions for which we had no answers. Our church agreed to help us, which overcame a big hurdle for us. Our biggest challenge was taking our two teenage girls with us and finding a good school for them to attend.

Our church had taught many lessons about walking by faith.

We had asked a few of our close Christian friends for advice without much success, because our church did not have any veteran missionaries.

Some ministries can be planned and talked about, and others need to be modeled. This was one of those. I'm sure many individuals have gone into ministries because it was a desire of their hearts and achieved success, but we had decided we needed to hear from heaven if this would work for us. After much prayer and overcoming numerous trials, it became clear to us that this was what the Lord wanted us to do, so in 1984, we returned to Brazil.

In June of 1990, we received notice that our church in Anderson was dissolving, and another church was taking over. They would pay for our plane fare back to Indiana before the transfer took place. This was a shock to us as we talked about our next move. The Spirit quickened us to understand it was the will of the Lord that had chosen Brazil for us, and our church was there to help us get it done. The Lord revealed to us if we would stay and continue the work, we would be a blessing, and we would be blessed in return. The choice was ours. We chose to stay in Brazil, and yes, we have been blessed.

Living and working in Brazil for a time triggered our memories of what had happened in Anderson during the 1970 outpouring of the Holy Spirit in our region. It was as if we had lived in a dimness before the sun rose and then something turned on the light gradually until it became brighter day by day. There was a hunger for the Word of God; the spiritual gifts were liberally given; miracles were common. The supernatural power of the Spirit was like a tidal wave sweeping over the land, and we were living in it without a clear understanding of why. We knew it was the sovereign power of the Spirit moving in our region, and it was good. Our calling to Brazil was birthed under this move of the Spirit of God, and our arrival in Rio ushered us in under this bold powerful move of the Spirit in every place we ministered without us knowing it.

Every meeting we attended was filled with hungry hearts and there was a joy that filled the room with tears and hope. We invited those who wanted to join this army to give their hearts to the Lord. We discovered that many were disappointed in the leadership of the past who made promises and did not deliver. Since our arrival on December 26, 1984, we could feel the spiritual climate increasing. As time passed, there was a Spirit-induced hunger, and expectations were increasing without a known or visible cause. A hunger was growing in the region, and we were in the middle of it without knowing why.

4

The Giant Called Brazil

As our meetings continued to grow, we could see there were hundreds of people looking for real hope. One of the visions the Spirit showed us was a huge ripe harvest of souls in Brazil, people who had heard the Word and believed what they had heard but had not acted upon that truth. Our job was to stir up what was already there, motivating hungry hearts to step out in faith and be led by the Spirit to do the work of the Lord—not just *hear*, but also *do*.

The Spirit gave me a vision of a giant man who was asleep on a beach. Suddenly large hands appeared and began to shake the giant to wake him up. He sat up, looked around, and stood up. He was a huge man, muscular and strong, and I could hear a voice saying, "Wake up, stand up on your feet, and become that leader that heaven has desired you to become."

The giant began to look around, and his eyes were fixed on a large dark cloud in the sky, called corruption, covering the land. The same voice said, "I will remove this curse from over my people," and the sunlight began to brighten the entire country. I woke up from the vision mystified as to the meaning, and I heard a voice say to me, "That giant is Brazil, a country that I love, but the forces of darkness have blinded the leaders to follow the wrong pathway called corruption, deceit, and bribery. I have chosen to revive this giant and use him to be a blessing to his people and the world. Go and tell my people I love them, I love their country, and revival will cover their land."

The changes we see today, I saw forty years ago.

God answers prayers.

His Word tells us that we have not because we do not ask Him. When we began to see the fruit that our ministry was producing, we were blessed, but we were not yet sure the message of the Kingdom was producing lasting change in the churches and the people. The children we began with were now teenagers, and they still had a hunger for the truth. Whenever we ministered and called for those who wanted help from heaven and to receive Jesus to come forward and receive, there were many new faces with tears, lifting their voices to the Lord.

As I look back, one young woman's story stands out. She was in her late twenties, and she had a sad look on her face. She told us that all her female friends were married and had children. She felt left out. We spoke to her about God's plan for men and women, marriage, and families, and that the Lord had not forgotten her request. We were surprised to find out she had never asked the Lord for that special someone in her life. She said that God was too busy to hear her request. After we helped straighten out her wrong thinking, we prayed with her, and she opened her heart and gave voice to her needs. The following year we returned to that city and that church. While we were in a minimart, she recognized us and called out to us. She could not wait to tell us how

God had answered her prayer as she introduced a handsome young man who smiled at us and hugged her. They told us they were married and expecting their first child. He had been waiting for the right woman. The young woman was hoping, and not long after she had prayed with us, they met, dated, and were soon married. We have so many stories like this one of prayers answered when we obey the Word of God.

Tithing is ten percent of what the Lord gives us.
As we developed methods to teach biblical truths to our new converts, we had to find ways to teach tithing. Even though tithing is not new to church members, very few Christians know or understand the history of the tithe—giving back ten percent, which began under the old covenant and continued in the new— as support for the physical building where the believer worships, support for the pastor, outreach to the lost, and local and foreign missions. There is a promise from God written in His Word (Malachi 3) that when we tithe, His blessing will rest upon us and our family. In some of the churches, many people did not know that this promise was in God's Book, the Bible. After they implemented this principle, they could see God's blessings begin to flow not only in money but in resources, new members, and growth.

Bible studies became our outreach.
Home Bible studies were one of our most successful outreaches. People with different beliefs would invite us to have a Bible study in their homes and hear about the five-fold ministry and gifts for the church. The traditional church did not teach or practice these giftings of the Spirit for the church. Apostles, prophets, teachers,

miracles, help, healing, and administration were special gifts for leaders only. We teach that any Spirit-filled Christian can be used by the Lord to bless the church as the Spirit desires. And we taught that the Holy Spirit is the one who will distribute and manifest the gifts as He wills.

Ministering to the ministers

Many of the seminaries did not teach biblical truth about satan and his demon activity, so very few were Spirit-filled. We developed relationships with pastors and their families, and we found ourselves ministering to the needs of these servants. Many felt secure in confessing oppression and burnout, and spiritual, mental, and physical attacks. Some of them asked us if we would give their church two Sundays of ministry while they took some time off to be spiritually restored. And when they returned, we could see the difference. That time off was a blessing for them.

We found out that among the leaders, wolves are looking for an opportunity to steal or influence the leadership of the church. When we began our work, these flaws were not visible. Every church leader had a smile and kind words, but with some, there was a hidden agenda. The gifting of the Spirit was a blessing for us and those we were helping, especially words of knowledge and discerning demon spirits. We had no way of knowing how these giftings were helping the churches.

Praying for the president of Brazil

The country was holding an election for the next president as they moved from military rule to civilian. The people were excited to vote for a civilian leader after years of military rule. During our times of prayer, we heard the Spirit say, "Pray for the leader," so we did. As time for the election came near, one of the most popular candidates became ill and underwent many surgeries. The churches prayed for his recovery, and eventually he passed away, which shocked the nation. As we prayed, we asked the Lord what had happened to this leader. Did we not pray correctly for his recovery? The Lord responded that He gave us the assignment to pray for the presidency, not the man who had passed away. The vice president became the leader the Lord chose to lead the change after military rule.

We are not doing this for money or fame.

We were getting invitations to speak in many churches, and the pastors welcomed us to help people receive the Lord, but we could sense that a few of them were not sincere. We did not want that mark on our ministry. So, we prayed and asked the Lord to stop any invitations from getting to us that were not His will for us. Within a month, the invitations were down to about half the number they had been before, but we saw more salvations and people being filled with the Spirit, which taught us discernment in this area of church life.

The Spirit is a wise farmer.

During our stay in the southern regions, the Lord did more through us. We met missionaries from England who were teaching small farmers how to improve the use of their land. We had an opportunity to get the farmers saved and filled with the Spirit of God. News traveled fast in rural areas as we prayed for the sick, cast out demons, and saw church attendance double. We were called upon to give counsel in church matters and disagreements much like the early church in the Book of Acts.

Women who could not have babies would come to the church services for prayer, and the Holy Spirit would do the impossible for them.

Many Brazilians were born into and raised in spiritism and other false beliefs that tormented them when they came to Christ. Sometimes we would meet people from other belief systems and try to engage them in conversation just to try and understand what they teach, which wasn't much. Many did not know they had been influenced by spiritism, voodoo, or witchcraft, and they needed to be freed from these.

Denominational divisions

Most Brazilian evangelical churches were started by other established churches in Europe, Scandinavia, England, and the US. The denominational doctrines of those churches were embedded in the fabric of the new churches in Brazil. The main church of Brazil was patterned after the doctrinal understanding from the thirteenth century. As the church grew, new revelations developed from then until the church of modern times. The Holy Spirit warned us to not get entangled in denominational differences, family arguments, political disputes, or religious arguments. We thank God for His guidance and for revealing to us that we were there to help where we could.

Revelation, dreams, and words of knowledge

The best times of learning from the Spirit were after a meeting with the leaders of the Mission or churches. After preaching in a church and praying for the needs of the people afterward, it seemed to me that the Holy Spirit would cause my thoughts to go over what had come out of my mouth with what should have been said, for clarity and edification. Many times, the revelation was short and to the point, and other times it was a complete rehashing of my message. As I look back upon that time, I can see that I was being taught as I was teaching others. I always prayed before speaking to different churches or groups, and most of the time the Spirit was guiding the listener to the ministry of Jesus. From time to time, I could sense that I was speaking exactly what needed to be said. Sometimes, I would miss the mark completely and improve the next time I spoke. Like a student teacher learning to teach, I learned through this process.

I believe that many of our dreams are previews of things to come. I also believe that if we ask the Lord about our dreams, the Holy Spirit will reveal deep meanings to us. When our family moved to Brazil, and we had developed a routine for us as a family, the Lord began to give us dreams and understanding about Mission Volantes de Cristo. What were its goals, the ultimate purpose for its existence, to do what, how, and why? The dreams we received answered questions for us and the leadership. We did not have a clear understanding of what the Lord was showing us until we asked Him about small problems that would have serious consequences if not attended to as soon as possible.

Without a complete understanding of the working of the Spirit, we did receive what heaven was saying but not how it would affect the future of the Mission. As we look back, we thank God for the many dreams and revelations He gave us on our journey. His unlimited knowledge, grace, and wisdom can work miracles.

5

Solutions for the Mission

There were issues inside the Mission that needed to be resolved, corrections that needed to be made. The Holy Spirit revealed why some of the finances were drying up at that time though the leadership did their best to remedy those problems.

The Spirit gave me this vision for the leaders. I saw a railroad track with a train moving forward. As it traveled, it came to a place where someone had installed a switch to a parallel track that would cause the train to switch to another track going in the same direction but gradually veering off the original direction. I asked the Lord what this vision meant to me or the Mission or our work in Brazil. He revealed to me that the first track was the will of the Lord for the Mission, which they had followed from the beginning, establishing evangelical churches where there were none. On that road, they had places to work and rest, resources, and finances. But the enemy had caused a switch track to be inserted into their work to get the Mission on a parallel track doing work other than what the Lord had given them. When I gave them that revelation, they could not believe it. Their question was, what do we do now? The answer from the Spirit was to go back to the place where they changed away from their original work, God's plan and purpose. Do that original plan until the Lord gives you something else or different. They looked at what they had been doing when they allowed changes to be made. When they changed back to the original plans God had given them, things began to go forward again.

Brazilian missionary training school

The Mission had a school that taught basic evangelism, which was mandatory for all the candidates to go into the mission field. Our working in the school allowed us to talk with all the students and hear what motivated them to choose mission evangelism as their ministry.

We soon outgrew the Mission's schedule for us as the calling of the Lord and the Spirit kept opening doors for us.

From this volunteer work in the school came invitations to minister in churches. We soon outgrew the Mission's schedule for us as the calling of the Lord and the Spirit kept opening doors for us. In small cities and towns, news gets around by word of mouth, and many of the invitations we received were from people we had never met who had heard about our ministry.

During that first year in Brazil, the Holy Spirit guided us to where we should go. Our job was to help with spiritual and physical know-how in different areas of work. My wife and I were born-again Spirit-filled Christians with more than ten years of experience in starting and running a small business, plus I grew up working in my grandfather's garage and gas station. I had been taught how to fix things—mechanical, gas-powered, or electrical. I was at home with those kinds of things. God knew this long before we had figured out why Brazil. He had called and commissioned us, filled us with His Spirit, and caused us to be in the right place at the right time for the right reason.

We were sent on a mission, a mission given to us by the Lord. To accept or reject it was in our hands. The final decision was ours, but it was not easy. It required many days and weeks of prayer to discern God's will. We had been down this road a few times before, when we were deciding to move from Chicago to Alabama and ended up in Indiana and when we decided to open a music store in Anderson, Indiana without any money, just faith. And when we expanded to a second and third store in Indianapolis, it was by faith. It became an adventure. The Lord said to us, "When I open a door for you, go through it, because it will be My will for you." Many doors began to open to us, and we saw victory after victory in people's lives. When people were filled with the Spirit, good things began to happen. The gifts of the Spirit manifested in almost every place we ministered the Word.

Dying churches

My bus rides from Seropedica to Rio gave me time to study how small towns, shopping centers, and churches worked in Brazil. On one of these trips, I saw this large traditional church with vultures on the roof. This was the first time I had seen a sight like this. As I wondered about what I was seeing, I heard the Spirit say, "This is one of the issues here. The churches that were once alive with people and activity are spiritually dead now." I thought to myself, *Dead, yes, dead. Absent of vision or life.* I asked the Lord what I could do to revive what I was seeing—the places and the people. "Tell them the Good News and the work of the Spirit and show them that Jesus is still alive in every believer."

That was when the Spirit revealed that revival was in the air and would soon manifest in many churches and cities and wake up those dead places of worship. A short time later, the doors of churches that had been closed to us began to open.

6

Help from Heaven

The Mission had many teams that worked at various tasks to get things done. We served on a team that was to drive a van loaded with the Mission's mobile kitchen utensils and furniture to a new location. One of the Mission personnel was traveling with us, and he did not speak English. The trip should have taken about five hours on a full tank of fuel, which we had. Three hours passed with no difficulties. Then we heard a loud noise. We stopped to look at the motor, which was in the rear, and discovered that our fan belt had broken. The VW was air-cooled, and the fanbelt drove the cooling fan that kept the engine cool.

This happened in the middle of nowhere on a Sunday. There was almost no traffic on the highway, and it was at a time when the military was in control of the nation, and all the gas stations were prohibited from opening on Sundays. So, we prayed for help, and I felt the Spirit give me peace that this was not a problem but a challenge. We kept telling our Brazilian brother that this was not a problem, and he looked at us as if we were from another planet. We had a few tools, so I cut what was left of the belt and cleaned up the debris when a thought came to me that we could drive until the engine was near overheating, cut the engine off, and coast until we stopped. We were on a hilly road, so we tried this idea, which worked for about ten miles. Then we coasted until the motor cooled enough for us to go again to the next town, where we found an open repair shop that had a belt that fit our minivan. We paid a mechanic for his work, used the balance of our financial resources for illegal fuel, and continued to the mission site.

After asking a few people directions to the location we were looking for, on a mountain that used all the fuel we had, we found ourselves in the dark and only halfway to our destination. Our Brazilian partner was about to have a fit when we told him it was no problem. We put on our four-way flashers, and he and I stood behind the van, waving to the other cars to go around us. After about thirty minutes, a car pulled up behind us. The driver opened its trunk, pulled out a gas can, and began to pour gasoline into our minivan. When he was finished, he replaced the can in his car and drove off. We never saw his face; he never said a word, while we were standing behind the minivan. We were shocked in amazement. We started the van and drove to the city on top of that mountain, rejoicing and puzzled.

After our third year of living in Brazil, we had a brief period of rest back at our church in Anderson, Indiana. One of our supporters in Anderson gave us a computer for our ministry, and we had difficulty bringing it back to Rio. At that time, the authorities did not allow foreign-manufactured personal computers to be brought into the country. We were informed that the computers would be confiscated and not returned to the owner.

I created this clandestine idea for our return journey to Rio through Paraguay via a Paraguay airline and then continue by bus. We would cross the border in Foz de Iguacu in Brazil and take another bus to Rio. We had taken that trip once before with no problem, so I thought it would be easy. We followed our plan until we took the bus to Rio. About an hour into our trip, the federal police stopped our bus for an inspection, which happens all the time. Many of the street vendors from Rio use this route to purchase items that cannot be bought in Brazil to sell in the city. That kind of inspection was common, with officers searching mainly for drugs. All the luggage was removed and inspected before it was reloaded.

About half an hour later, two of the police boarded the bus, holding our computer and asking who it belonged to. I raised my hand, and they asked me to follow them outside and began to ask me a lot of questions. I was informed that they would have to keep the computer because it was on their list of items not allowed in the country. As I waited, they asked me why I needed a computer. I explained that I was documenting my trip. I told them, if it was illegal, they could take it; I needed it, but I could live without it. With my reply, they closed it up and returned it to the luggage compartment.

The Spirit warned us to not get entangled in corruption of any kind, so I was not going to pay money to keep that computer. When the police saw I was not going to become a part of their plan, they returned the computer to the luggage compartment.

A third of school tuition paid—a miracle!
After we had lived in Brazil for six months, the Lord opened the door for our middle daughter, Paula, to return to Indiana and graduate with her high school class.

Our youngest daughter attended the American school in Rio for three years on scholarships, which was a big help to us. Her final semester, no scholarships were available, and the tuition was overdue. We did not have the funds to pay all the fees, so we asked the Lord for help. We discovered that the Lord has hundreds of ways to help his people when they ask, and he will make a way out of no way. We needed an extra fifty dollars a month to cover everything, but we did not have a way to get it.

During our time in Rio, we had become friends with many of the other English-speaking missionaries working in Rio and other places in Brazil. One of the couples came up with the idea of us getting together once a month for an evening of prayer and praise in English. Most of our work and contacts were in Portuguese, which is the language of Brazil.

After many of these meetings, the leaders would add something new and different to our time together. At one meeting, following our normal time singing and praising, the leader asked each couple to stand up and introduce themselves and tell what they did in Rio. The

We were not aware of how the Lord was using us to help other mission couples.

first couple he called on did what he asked; then two more couples gave their information. They added how we had helped them in a few situations and prayed for them and their teenagers. More than half of the others told how we had been instrumental in their lives and ministries. We were not aware of how the Lord was using us to help other mission couples.

We had invited a new pastor and his wife who were new to the area to go with us to this meeting. On our way back to our apartment, this new pastor told us that he and his wife had wanted to help a local work in Rio, and after hearing the testimonies that night at the meeting, they wanted to help us with our mission work in the poor neighborhoods of Rio. They committed to give us exactly fifty dollars every month, which paid for our daughter's tuition at the American School of Rio. When she graduated, the pastor and his wife headed back to the US, and the fifty dollars stopped. The Lord had supplied our need.

The Lord gave us places to live.

Our assignment was clear. We were to help this Mission achieve its goals and evangelize the cities the Lord opened to them. Our opposition came from some of the established mainline churches—denominational churches from Europe, the US, Scandinavia, and other Christian countries with a long history of Christian work.

We discovered that the longer we stayed, the more we loved the country, the people, and the culture. We overcame the change in climate, the bugs, the language, and food in our new home. We worked on the things we could first: school for the girls, a safe place to live. With the nearest telephone to the outside world a mile away, no television, McDonalds, or Pizza Hut, we all had to learn to adapt to our new normal, and that is not easy when you are in your forties—not impossible but challenging. Day by day, we overcame the obstacles that were before us while we helped our Brazilian family to adapt and live with the Americans.

The longer we stayed, the more we loved the country, the people, and the culture.

There are two types of time in Brazil: local Brazilian time and British/American time. We had to learn local time and customs;

we were on a mission with goals. As we learned more about Rio, we found a shortcut from the south side to the north, but we had to cross a few mountains and hills.

Our daughters had met the daughter of another American family that lived near the school. This family owned an apartment for rent, and we were able to rent it and move from Seropedica to a suburb closer to the school called the Barra Sul Tijuca. Our apartment was on an upper floor, and we tried to keep a low profile, not wanting to attract attention to ourselves. This location was great for us until Dara graduated from high school and the apartment owner did not want to renew the lease.

We had begun to make inroads into a high-rise complex a few miles toward central Rio, and we were invited to a get-together in one of the condos. We were introduced to everyone, and we gave a short talk about why we were in Brazil. Afterward, something the Lord had previously revealed to us was going to happen in the future came to pass. We always asked if anyone had any needs we could pray for. There were always needs in families, marriages, children, and jobs. We were introduced to the hired help, and all of them wanted prayer, which we were glad to do.

The wife of the condo owner had a friend at this meeting who was having trouble with her feet, so we prayed for her, and the pain disappeared. She explained to us how she had attempted suicide and had broken her feet, so we began to dig in with questions to see if the Lord would reveal the cause of her depression. It was a demonic attack, which we broke. Then, after she accepted Jesus, we prayed for healing in her mind and freedom.

Our host told her we were looking for an apartment, and she interrupted to tell us she had an apartment in the next condo complex. She offered to show it to us that evening if we would like. We jumped at this open door, as the Lord had told us when a door opens to us, take it. After looking the place over, we asked how much it would cost to rent it, and she responded, "Nada," *nothing*. We were shocked, so we asked for how long and she said, "Para sempre" (*forever*), and she gave us the keys that night. She introduced us to the guards, explained the protocol and parking, and asked us for one thing: to pay the condo fee every month, which we did. We knew the Lord was in this, so we thanked and praised Him for this open door.

We could see clearly that when He wants you to get in any place, He will open the door, as He did so many times for us. This was an open door, and as we looked back, we could see that the Spirit of God was guiding our footsteps to the places He wanted us to go. From Seropedica to a rented residence in Rio and now to Barra Sul, one of the costliest places on that side of the city, rent-free! Praise the Lord!

Our last place of residence in Brazil was Curitiba. A mission couple we met in language school needed someone to occupy their residence while they went to the US for a furlough. We moved into their home for the time they would be away without knowing that this city would be our next assignment.

7

God Unlocks Gasoline Caps

After we moved from Seropedica to Barra, I still had to travel back to Seropedica to teach. Twice a week, I drove one hour from Barra to Seropedica, stayed overnight, and returned to Barra the next day. On one of these trips, I discovered that my fuel was low, so I stopped at a gas station and discovered I had misplaced the key to the car's gas cap. I asked the attendant if the station had any old fuel caps with keys so maybe I could unlock my gas cap, and he said he didn't think so, but he would look in the office.

While he was inside, I could see that I was going to be late, but I couldn't make it without more fuel. I prayed for my gas cap and thanked the Lord for it to open. I tried the ignition key, and it went in, and the cap opened. I was shocked. When the attendant returned to my car, I stood laughing beside my vehicle with the cap in my hand. As he was filling my tank he asked where I found the key. I informed him that I didn't find it; I used the ignition key. He said no way; that was impossible because the ignition key and gas cap keys are not the same. I stood in front of him, holding the gas cap with the ignition key in it. I told him I was a Christian, that I prayed and asked for help, and then tried the ignition key and it worked. I replaced the cap when he was finished, paid him, and told him God did this. Then I drove off, leaving him with a strange look on his face. I was thankful that I was going to arrive at the Mission with time to spare, but I was still puzzled over this miracle, so I looked for a place to pull off the road and verify what had just happened. I pulled off the road, took the ignition key to the fuel cap, and tried to open it. The key would not even go into the slot. I heard the Spirit say, "This worked because you needed it and prayed." The Word of the Lord came to me: "Ye have not because ye ask not" (James 4:2 KJV).

God heals feet.
At one of the churches we worked with, a man and his family were seeking help and told us this story about their daughter. She would cry and beg her parents to take her to a doctor who could surgically fix her feet to be tiny and shaped like the Japanese dancers she had seen. Her request created a serious problem in their home, and her father told her they would try to find a doctor who could do surgery like that. They met with a doctor who informed them that this was possible, but once completed, the surgery could not be reversed. Their daughter said she understood that, but she still wanted to have the surgery anyway, so they agreed, and their daughter jumped for joy. The surgeries took a year to complete. After she recovered from the surgery, she began to have severe pain in her feet and ankles, to the point that she could not walk. The family had become Christians and asked for prayer to reverse what had been done. We joined them in prayer, asking the Lord to repair this wrong choice. About a year later, we returned to that church and family to minister and find out what happened, and the couple gave us an update. The Lord

took away most of the pain in her feet and ankles, and she could walk again, but the tiny feet she had asked for would remain with her the rest of her life.

Burning Bibles?

My wife and I were invited to travel to a city in southern Brazil near the border with Paraguay. The Mission leader had friends in the city he wanted us to meet, and from that meeting, we were asked to attend a gathering of church leaders who were meeting for various reasons and events in the city. One of the pastors told this story about the Gideons passing out New Testament Bibles to young people in the Catholic grade school. The next day the local priest called a meeting in the school and explained that they were Catholic. The Bibles were Protestant Bibles and were not good for them to read. He wanted every youngster who had received a Protestant Bible from the Gideons to bring it to school the next day and turn it in or risk being excommunicated from the church.

The next day, after he had collected the Bibles, he piled them in the school courtyard, set them on fire, and burned them for all to see. After that report and a few others, I was asked to speak about revival. I was speaking through a translator, and when I tried to speak on revival, it would not flow. The subject the Holy Spirit gave me was holy indignation about the Protestant Bible incident. I could not believe that in 1985 such a thing could be done and not be challenged in a Christian nation. I told them I had read about a few accounts of this happening in rural northern regions of Brazil years ago, but it was difficult to believe it could happen today. I asked them to forgive me for not speaking on revival, but I could not let this go. I said, "I am not a Brazilian, so I have no power in your country, but you do. I want to speak about

45

denominational differences in the church," which I did. When all evangelical churches have the same goal—getting the lost and hurting saved and healed—we are all on the same team. When I finished, I took my seat, and the room was so quiet it was spooky. The leader stood up to speak, saying, "The Americanos are right. We must do something about this."

On our last day there, one of the pastors gave us this account of what happened later. A group of pastors requested to meet with the Catholic leader in the city to discuss this. The same group requested a meeting with the mayor to inform him about this issue. The following day an apology was given to this group of pastors and the city for what that priest had done. I was never invited back to that city, but I have no regrets. The Lord opened so many other cities to us that it did not matter to us.

Blind eyes opened

We were invited to join another pastor evangelist for a weekend of preaching and prayer in a small town near Campinas. I was still struggling with preaching in Portuguese, and I explained this to the pastor who asked me to go with him. After arriving in a small city not too far from Campinas, we began to evangelize from house to house, a practice I was familiar with.

After a one-day door-to-door evangelizing campaign and inviting the people to come to the church that was the principal sponsor, we invited those we spoke with to the church meeting the following night. A huge crowd showed up for that meeting, and the leader preached. Afterward, we prayed for the people's needs. The leader informed me that the following night, I was scheduled to preach, but we did not have an interpreter for me. They made calls to everyone they knew but with no success. I did have a friend in Campinas, but he had a commitment for the following night. He told me he had a friend who might serve as an interpreter if he was available that night, and he would let me know. The next day I received a phone call from a seminary student who agreed to help us, so we exchanged information on the time and place of the meeting. When he arrived that evening, we talked with him and his wife for a brief period so he could understand my voice and accent and the text I would be using that evening. His wife was an American, and we had a chance to talk for a while and answer a few questions. I was a bit nervous and so was he, but the message found good ground and was on time.

The Holy Spirit guided us when I offered a general prayer for those who were suffering from sickness, disease, or infirmity. There was a woman standing near the front who began to shout with her hands held high. She began to scream something I could not understand, and everyone who was seated stood up and began to praise the Lord and shout and sing. I asked the pastor what was going on, and he said that she was blind and now she could see. He told us she had been blind for years so this was a miracle, and all who knew her were rejoicing. The church erupted with praise and thanksgiving that went long into the night.

An open door to Campinas

After the event, I had a chance to thank my interpreter for his help in translating for me, and that opened the door to Campinas for us. He invited me to visit his church in Campinas, so after our revival meeting was completed, I accepted his invitation and visited his home church, realizing this was a God-ordained connection between us and the Agape church in Campinas. He introduced me to his family, and I could feel the anointing of the

Spirit, but I wasn't sure what to do next. After all, these were Spirit-filled adults working in the church. I was motivated to ask them if I could pray for them, and they agreed. I proceeded, and the Spirit gave me a strong and clear revelation over each of them. I knew the Lord was doing something in this family and the church, and I wanted to be a part of whatever the Lord was doing. This began a thirty-year relationship for us in that city plus six other cities affiliated with the Agape network of churches.

8

Demons Must Go

During our first year of ministry, we would pray for people in their homes and with their families. We did not know that many of the people in our area were practicing spiritism, witchcraft, and voodoo. An urgent call came to the Mission for help for a young woman tormented by a demonic presence. We paid a visit to her home, where many believers had gathered. After asking a few questions, we asked the girl if she wanted to be free of this evil attack. Then we led her to the Lord and broke the power of darkness over her life. The girl's father and his entire family became Christians that night, confessing Jesus as Lord and Savior. We asked if they had any spiritism images in their home and if they did, we asked them to destroy them as quickly as possible if they wanted to stay free.

We discovered that numerous homes and families were tormented by demons, and those people were seeking relief. Many of them were believers in Christ but had no power to stop the evil powers of darkness. Many Christians and non-believers had been taught methods of how to deal with the darkness of spiritism. We could see that the Lord had opened this door of ministry for us, and we were excited to be invited to Bible studies, church meetings, and gatherings of all types to shed light on the power of the Holy Spirit's ministry of warfare.

We were learning Portuguese, but we still needed to work through Brazilian interpreters wherever we went to speak. So, all my messages had to be short and compact. With two people preaching, this kind of ministry was slow. We did not know how long we would stay in Brazil because the Lord had not yet revealed that to us. We did not have a large organization behind our church and the mission. Following the guidance of the Holy Spirit, we witnessed victory in many lives. In the middle of all these events, the Lord did not allow confusion or fear to stop what He was doing through us. Our mission was to preach the Word, pray for the sick and tormented, and break demonic holds on families, churches, and ministries of God's Word. These encounters were our introduction to Brazilian culture.

A family affair

Our interpreter asked if we could pray for a relative of his who needed help. We agreed and went to the person's apartment. The husband and father of this family told us this story of how he had become violent and out of control in their home and wanted help. When we arrived, there was a small group of friends and neighbors there, and we were surprised that so many people were there waiting to see what would happen. After introductions were made, we asked the man and his wife if we could converse with them alone, and they agreed, so we went to their bedroom. The husband told us he was trying to get a promotion at his job, and he decided to ask the help of a spiritist center that instructed him to make a sacrifice to one of their gods. So he did, and everything went crazy in his head. He became violent and began fighting with his wife, who was pregnant. He kicked her in the stomach, and she began to hemorrhage with pain. We explained to them that God could help them, but they must renounce whatever spirit he had received and give his life and family to Jesus. As we began to pray for the husband, the spirit in him started to resist. His eyes became glassy, and his face twisted with a snarl. As we led him to confess Jesus as his Lord, the spirit resisted, and he began to levitate off the floor, and he lunged at me. It happened so fast that I could not react quickly enough, so I just stared at him as he came at me. He hit an invisible barrier in front of me, and he fell to his knees growling. I pressed in with prayer in the Spirit and told him to say the name of Jesus. When he finally broke through and confessed the name of Jesus, whatever it was let him go, and he began to weep and cry out and confess that he was sorry for what he had done to his wife and family. His wife followed his lead and made her confession of Jesus, and they both began to smile and weep. We led them in a prayer dedication of their family and home to the Lord. We prayed for the hemorrhage to stop and for her body to be healed.

As we came out of the bedroom with both smiling, the people in the next room were bewildered and wanted to know what had happened. We interrupted the questions and asked if anyone else wanted prayer. Their housekeeper was the first one in line for prayer, and as we prayed over her, she began to shake and fell to the floor and began to slither like a snake. We knew it was an unclean spirit, so we commanded it to let her go and never return. Our interpreter was a female, and she had never seen a deliverance before, so when the spirit came out, she was on her toes dancing around in fear for what she was seeing. After we helped the housekeeper up and led her in prayer, she informed us that she had been saved and filled with the Spirit years ago but had fallen into spiritism. She had two children, was not married, and was sleeping around. We broke that demonic hold over her life. We prayed for everyone who asked and led them to the Lord.

Before we left, our interpreter told us a story of how another pastor had come to help the man we had prayed for and how the spirit jumped on him and chased him out of their home. The group that was there had come to see what was going to happen to these Americans, not expecting to see the power of the Holy Spirit in action.

South African connection in Rio

One of the pastors we worked with extended to us an invitation to attend a diplomatic celebration for the independence of the nation of South Africa. I was not interested in attending this celebration because I respected Nelson Mandela, who was imprisoned at the time for standing up for his people. The next morning, I heard the Spirit say, "Go to this event," so Cynthia and I went.

In a large ballroom at the South African consulate, the official in charge of the guests explained the reason for the event with countries and churches actively working in South Africa. We were introduced to a few of the diplomats and church leaders from other African countries and felt a little out of place. We were introduced to many embassy workers as we walked around praying for whatever the Lord wanted to do, looking for an opportunity. One of the church leaders we had met earlier escorted us to a woman we did not know and introduced her to us as the consulate's wife. After the introduction, she asked us about the work we were doing in the poor areas of Rio. We could see she had been drinking and was a little tipsy. Somehow, she was interested in how we looked so young and had become successful in violent areas of the city and wanted to know how long we had lived in Rio. She was curious and wanted to know our ages and seemed surprised when we told her. Then she made this statement of how "you people hold your appearance so well."

We could have become offended by her statement, but I felt that the Lord wanted us to witness to her. So, I told her that our appearance had very little to do with our race or color and a lot to do with knowing Jesus. Her face changed as if I had slapped her. She quickly thanked us and dismissed herself.

We could have become offended by her statement, but I felt that the Lord wanted us to witness to her.

The rest of the evening was good, because we learned a lot about the diamond-producing countries in Africa. We came to realize that the consulate's wife was the reason we were there. The Holy Spirit caused us to understand the two kinds of people in Brazil and the world at large: those who are down and out and others who are up and out. He said, "I love them all, and they need My help."

Keep your eye on the goal.
During five years of ministry in Rio and its nearby cities like Vitoria, Fortaleza, Campinas, and Sao Paulo, and many churches and Bible studies, the Spirit of God continually reminded us to push all distractions out of our way and stay on the road of revival in Brazil. Many opportunities came our way to do other things,

which could have been good for us and the churches and pastors we were working with, but these things were not the will of God for us. I would like to say it was easy, but it was not. We had to resist the mental struggle and temptation through prayer and the help of the Holy Spirit.

The calling of the Lord can be multiple for some and singular for others. Through trial and error, we discovered that our calling was Brazil. The important people we were meeting and the invitations to speak at various conferences that lifted the faith of pastors and other missionaries were too important to be a coincidence. Open doors to churches in other states and cities and the obvious anointing of the Spirit gave us assurance we were on the right track. The Holy Spirit gave us victories in battles we did not fight. We prayed daily for the things the Spirit revealed to us, but sometimes we walked into a battle already won. The word of the Lord to us was, "Do not start a new church in Brazil. You are in Brazil to help those churches that hear my voice and follow my will. I will supply all your needs above and beyond what you can believe." He did then and continues to do so.

We were able to resolve disagreements in churches or Bible study groups. There is a name that is above every name. "Therefore God also has highly exalted Him and given Him the name which is above every name, that at the name of Jesus every knee should bow, of those in heaven, and of those on earth, and of those under the earth" (Philippians 2:9-10 NKJV).

9

Transportation Provided

When we first arrived from the US and were living at the Mission leader's home, I noticed a nice-looking car propped up on concrete blocks in his yard, so I asked him what the problem with it was, and he told me it had many. I asked if I could look at it, and he gave his permission. I did a standard checkup of the battery, spark plugs, distributor, and fuel pump and couldn't find anything wrong. So, after charging the battery and putting fuel in the tank, I got it running. While the tires were being fixed, I cleaned it out, and we went for a ride and a wash.

It belonged to the Mission and became the Mission's only running vehicle. After a time, I did the same for the other vehicles until we had them all working as we prepared to go into the small-town areas to evangelize. About a month later, the leader of the Mission gave us our first car in Brazil for our personal use. We drove that car for almost three years before going home on our first furlough. I heard the Spirit say, "Give that car to one of the leaders before you leave." I did, and upon our return, he asked me if I wanted it back. I told him, "No, it's your car now. God will give us another one," and He did.

One of the visiting teachers was a retired Navy radio technician who spent a week teaching the history of the Christian church. He asked me if I would stay for his classes and intercede for him during his teaching time. He was good, and I prayed and listened to what he had to say. I learned a lot from him. I went home to our apartment in Barra Sul and told Cynthia about the guy, that we should keep him in prayer and that I was going back on Friday for his last class.

After his class, his company called and asked him to get back to the East Coast as soon as possible. The company had booked a first-class flight for him that night and expected him to be in New York the next morning. I helped him get to the airport with plenty of time for his flight. We talked for a while, and he told me he had a dream about what was happening with his flight back to the US and that he was to give me all the cash he had left before he boarded his plane. He handed me a wad of bills, shook my hand, and with a big hug went to his boarding gate. I was shocked and overjoyed by the offering and rejoiced all the way home. When I told Cynthia, the first thing she asked was how much. I didn't know because I had not counted the money. So, we counted it together. It was $1,800, and we cried for joy and gave thanks and praise to the Lord for doing what He said He would do. He supplied us with money for another vehicle to replace the one we had given to the other missionary when we left for furlough in the US.

Helping our daughter get a job

Now that we had our transportation, we found an apartment closer to the school that belonged to a family that had two girls who went to the same school as our daughter, and they offered this apartment to us for almost no cost. Our ministry was growing, so we tried to keep a low profile, which was nearly impossible in the area where we lived.

Our daughter wanted to get a job so she could get the things most teenagers want. We did not have extra money for those things. She asked if she could work after school and earn money teaching English. There were many language schools near us, and Dara had approached the manager of a school not very far from where we lived. The woman asked to talk with me, and I agreed.

When we met, she explained that she could not hire Dara because of her age and status. Dara was too young and not Brazilian. Then she proposed that what she could do, if I would agree to it, is hire me as a language coach for those who attended the school and hire Dara and pay her under my work for the school. I asked her if this was legal, and she told me it was and that they did it all the time with French and American coaches. I asked a few detailed questions about the time commitment required for me to do the coaching she needed.

Souls won to the Kingdom

After filling out the necessary papers, I asked her if she belonged to a local church. She did, and we discovered she and her family were members of the same church we attended when we were not out of town doing ministry in other cities. She also told me that she and her husband dropped their two boys off at the church, but they did not attend. I looked her in the eyes and told her, "You take those boys to church and stay in church to listen to what's being said."

She wanted to know what denomination I belonged to, and she did not see any use for what the pastor had to say. From that conversation, a new door opened for us to lead her and her family to the Lord, and over time we led almost all the teachers from the school to the Lord.

God produces electric power.

One of our other teams was in a city where the church did not want the evangelical message preached, which was common in the interior states of Brazil. The main church did not want other churches to be set up in small towns.

The work of the Mission was to enter a town, let the authorities know who they were and why they were there, and get permission to do open-air meetings in the town square. Then we would divide up into three-person teams and visit every house in the town to introduce the Mission there and invite them to the meeting that night. We would ask if they had any needs we could pray for: sickness, problems in families or the town. The people were curious and suspicious of our motives, but a few of them would openly ask for prayer and promise to come to the meeting that evening.

A priest confronts our Mission.

On one occasion, our team was confronted by the local priest to stop doing what we were doing, and our leader let him know that the Mission had every right to evangelize according to Brazilian laws. On that encounter, the priest slapped him. Our team member did not respond but just stared at the priest and then turned his face to the other cheek, and the priest slapped him again. He turned his cheek back to the other side, and the priest was about to slap him again when a few of the men from the town stepped in and restrained him. They told the priest that what he was doing was not right, and the priest turned and walked away.

That night the town square was filled with curious people singing along with the Mission's music group and waiting for what was next.

The Mission would usually do a short theatrical play of one of the Bible stories about salvation and then proceed with more singing and praise. After several more songs, one of the local men asked if he could say something, which we allowed. He told the assembly that he had been paid to disconnect the power supply in the town square in the middle of the service. He did that, but the amplifiers and microphones continued to function without interruption. He searched around the platform to see if any other power cord was connected and there was none. He called one of his friends to take the extension cord up to the platform and waved it for all to see. "How can this be?" he asked. "There is no other power supply to the square, yet the instruments continue to work." One of the leaders raised his hands toward heaven and began to praise the Lord. A hush came over the entire place as people began to weep and lift their hands toward heaven, praising the Lord for his blessings upon this meeting as our team members began to pray for the sick and hurt. Many lives were turned to the Lord that night.

We had adjusted ourselves to let new believers be baptized in the nearest church but when a person wanted to be baptized at once, we would use a swimming pool or the water in a local stream in rural cities. Cynthia and I began a Bible study for the teachers in the language school to assist them in their spiritual growth. On one occasion, one of the teachers who had a messed-up life gave her heart to the Lord and wanted to be baptized the same day. It was evening, and we asked her several times if it would be better to wait until a local church could baptize her on

Sunday. She wanted to know why not today. I could not think of a biblical reason why not. Cynthia asked her if she had shorts, pedal pushers, or a full bathing suit she could wear. After the women helped her get dressed, we all went down to a nearby beach where we baptized her. It was almost dark as we all waded out to waist-deep water and led her to a declaration and baptized her in the Atlantic Ocean on Barra Beach. She jumped up and down in the water, waving her hands and thanking Jesus for His great mercy and love.

About a month later we received a phone call from this same young woman asking for help. She explained to us that she and her live-in boyfriend had been arguing about her new life in Christ. He had been drinking and they had gotten into a fight, and she had used a razor knife and cut him. She asked if we could help her if the police showed up. We prayed over the phone and told her to be calm, as we were on our way.

When we arrived at her apartment, there was blood every-where. It was a mess, with blood on the furniture and the floor. Her boyfriend was sitting in a chair with blood on his face, mum-bling something incoherently. Cynthia was able to quiet the woman down and wash the blood from her face and hands as she explained what had happened between them and the fight during which she had cut him in the eye with a razor knife. When we lis-tened to his side of the story through his anger, we asked him if we could look at his eye, which looked normal to us. We asked if we could have a closer look by pulling the skin above the eye up, and his eyelid almost fell off in our hand.

As we attempted to wipe the blood away, Cynthia said she could not breathe and passed out, hitting her head on a table be-fore hitting the floor. I began to pray in the Spirit while I pulled

Cynthia over to an open window to get some air. The situation was almost out of hand: My wife was gasping for air on the floor with her head bleeding. The woman was hysterical with fear because if the police showed up to investigate, someone was going to jail. Her boyfriend was drunk and bloody, the apartment was a mess, and there were two Americans who spoke very little Portuguese involved in this.

The Lord answered our prayers with the help of a neighbor who agreed to allow the boyfriend to stay overnight. After the police arrived, she explained what had happened, and she and her boyfriend resolved the matter. After they left, I had to get Cynthia to a hospital or clinic and get that gash in her scalp attended to. We stopped by our apartment to get our daughter Dara before going to a hospital without the ability to explain what happened.

The next day, we met with our new convert and heard the end of the story. Everything had worked out. He did not lose his eyelid. He had received medical attention and was doing okay. In our attempts to help someone, the enemy came to do what he does—steal, kill, and destroy.

10

Cancer Healed

We prayed for a few members of the church we attended when we were not working in other cities. One of the American women we met at Union Church came under attack by a fear of dying after she was examined and cancer was discovered. The first challenge was to break off the spirit of fear, doubt, and unbelief over her mind. She had friends who had suffered the same infirmity, and some had died. She was given two choices by the doctors to eliminate the malignancy: surgery or radiation treatments. We were there to teach and encourage her to make the right choice, so we asked her what she believed the Lord would do for her. We prayed in agreement with her and ministered to her until the victory was won. The doctors administered radiation and shrank a lemon-sized tumor to the size of a small lump. She told everyone about what the Lord had done for her. We began to understand that we could teach about faith, but we could not cause a person to exercise faith in a life-and-death situation. We learned that on certain occasions, we needed to know what that person was believing and join them in prayer according to the written Word. God healed her completely.

He opens prison doors.

Our ministry continued to move forward to include those who were incarcerated. A mother asked us to visit her son who was locked up in prison. His mother had received Christ, and we joined her in praying for his release. After a brief inquiry, we were granted entry to visit inmates and distribute Bibles. Saturday was the only visitation day for family and friends to do this, so we went to various prisons once a month with no interference.

On one of these visitation days, we were surprised to find a large crowd outside the entry for visitors, so we asked if there was a problem. We were told that the warden had canceled all visits for that day because there had been an uprising the night before. We talked to a few of the other pastors we had met on other occasions to see what they were planning to do. I asked them to join us in prayer and ask the Lord for help to open the prison for visitors that day, as most of the visitors were women: mothers, wives, and girlfriends weeping because it was the only day they had free for prison visits. The pastors and other leaders smiled at our suggestion but joined in our prayer for the Lord to open the prison for us. Many of these women were Christians, so they joined in our prayer time, crying out to the Lord for help. Others just looked on as if this were an American sideshow.

After approximately an hour of prayer and singing, the guards opened the visitors' entrance without an explanation and began to check passes, allowing visitors to enter. When our turn came, we visited the man we came to see, and we asked him what had happened in the prison. He explained there had been a fight between two gangs and all visits were cancelled. He asked us what had happened outside, and we told him the Lord had opened the doors for all of us to come in. He could not believe what we were telling him. When he was released, he gave his heart to the Lord and joined one of the local churches.

Useless to useful

My wife and I were invited to intervene and pastor a church where the pastor had fallen into sexual relations with a woman in the church. The leadership and the pastor asked us to take over his duties until they could get a permanent pastor, which we did.

The pastor said he had arranged to baptize three people that coming Sunday and asked me to baptize them. They had been waiting for weeks. This was a confusing time, and I did not want to add to the confusion, so I agreed, and the following Sunday, we baptized them on their building's penthouse veranda in a child's wading pool.

The following week we agreed to meet with a few of the members who were having a rough time with the circumstances of their pastor's departure. One of these was a young man about thirty years old who told us his story. He got hooked on drugs when he was a teenager and fell into stealing, lying, prostitution, and everything that goes with street life. He was told many times that his problem was beyond help, so he decided to end his life by drug overdose. We asked him a few questions: "Do you want to live? Are you ready to try something different?" He responded yes. We asked him if we could pray for him, laid our hands upon his head and heart, and commanded the spirits of confusion, death, perversion, and drug addiction to leave his body in the name of Jesus. He began to tremble and shake and cry out in pain. When we asked him what he felt, with tears in his eyes he showed us his arms with needle injection marks everywhere. We commanded the pain to leave him as he asked the Lord into his life. Tears of joy replaced the marks of pain, and a smile came to his face as the Holy Spirit flooded his life.

When we asked him to receive the Holy Spirit and complete his deliverance from that life of the streets without Christ, he began to cry out for forgiveness and speak in tongues. He walked out of that office a new creation in Christ, and we all rejoiced over what the Lord had done during this church's time of confusion. We worked to help stabilize the church and attempt to save the couple's marriage. About two years later we met with a pastor and church leader who knew the young man who was delivered, and he gave us this account. After that day the young man met with us, he began to change and stayed drug-free, joined the church, enrolled in a Bible school, and met and married a Christian woman who knew him. They were expecting a child.

The Lord supplies food.
This came to us from one of the missionaries who was responsible for getting the mission house set up for the next incoming class. This house was near the beach. She used all the money that had been given to her and soon ran out of food. After two days of just bread and water, the team began to cry out in prayer for help, and the leader, who happened to be a female, went for a walk on the beach to talk with the Lord. As she was walking and pouring her heart out to the Lord, she could see what looked like a log on the beach a good distance away, so she walked faster. When she came near, she slowed down to try and figure out what it was that she was seeing. It was an alligator coming her way, so she went to the house to tell the others what she saw and for them to come and help her capture it. They killed it with big rocks and machetes, dragged it back to the house, and feasted for many days until the

other mission folk came. When they told the story and showed them the head and hide, the others began to shout for joy because there were no alligators in the rivers this far south. God had provided meat for them.

Heaven has gasoline.

We were asked to preach in a small town that was about sixty miles north of Rio. When the date arrived, we were in a difficult place, with only half a tank of fuel and no money. We had given our word that we would come, so we went, believing that the Lord would provide. The pastor and the church received us with open arms. We preached and prayed for every need in the church. The pastor had to leave for his other job, and he left one of his deacons with us to lock up after we left. After we prayed for the last person, the deacon walked with us to our car and then caught a bus home. I asked my wife, "Did anyone give you anything?" She said, "No, how about you?" We had a quarter of a tank of fuel, and it was getting dark, we didn't know anyone in that town, and we had a sixty-mile trip to where we were staying.

Then one of the parables Jesus told to his disciples came to me, so we laid our hands on the car and confessed our need for fuel enough to get us home, and we thanked the Lord and started for home. Cynthia was singing and praising the Lord, and I was watching our gas gauge when the Spirit told me, "Turn the dashboard lights off. The gas gauge is robbing your faith." So I did, and we arrived at the house where we were staying with no problem, rejoicing and praising the Lord.

The next morning, I was running late for a meeting in Rio, so I jumped in the car and started for Rio. About two blocks down the road, the motor began to stall and then stopped. I heard the

Spirit say to me, "You asked for enough fuel to get you home, not to go to Rio." Lesson learned. Whenever you pray, ask for more than enough. Heaven has plenty of whatever you need.

11

When Sickness Challenged Our Lives

The Lord healed us from many kinds of sicknesses that are common to Brazilians and deadly to Americans. Our ministry carried us into many areas that had mosquitoes that were deadly for us, and we had our share of mosquito and spider bites, especially in the interior and northern states.

We continually quoted the promise of the Lord recorded in Isaiah 53:5, "By his stripes we are healed." We are healed by what Jesus did for us on the cross. Whenever we came down with an illness that was new to us, we would pray the Word of God over that attack, rest, and in a few days, we would be back on our feet, healed. "He himself bore our sins" in His body on the cross, so that we might die to sins and live for righteousness; "by his wounds you have been healed"(1 Peter 2:24 NIV).

As we worked in different cities and towns teaching, praying, and showing the power of God, the enemy would attack in ways we had never experienced before. We used what we knew and recommendations from our Brazilian host, and the best part of this story is that the Lord healed us from every sickness or disease.

Learning to speak Portuguese

After three years of speaking through interpreters, we had to learn this language if we were going to stay in the country. So, we found a language school for missionaries in the city of Campinas. Working through a few of our friends in Rio, we were able to find lodging in Campinas, complete the application for the school, and continue the journey that the Lord opened to us. Our ministry time slowed as we completed the one-year training to speak and write Portuguese correctly. We began to receive more invitations from churches in the southern region of Brazil where we had little or no connections or interpreters.

While studying Portuguese in Campinas, we became friends with an American pastor and his family who were a big help to us in the city. It was in their church we were able to minister to Japanese believers, which was a blessing to us. They were a part of Revelation 14:6, "every nation and tongue." This pastor and his family helped us find housing while we attended language school. They also located a translator for us while we were working with another pastor on an evangelistic crusade near Campinas. We believe they were led by the Holy Spirit to assist us in so many other ways as the Lord opened to them in our missionary journey.

Wherever we traveled, we met and ministered to people with hearts hungry for God's biblical truths in His Word. It was amazing how the Lord would open doors to us in places we never expected. We had met many couples from different denominational churches that had sponsored them to work in Brazil. In talking with them, we found they could not believe we had come from a small nondenominational church and were able to work across denominational lines. They wanted to know how this could be, and our answer was that the Lord called us to do what we were doing, and He was providing for us. We would ask them questions like, "Aren't we all on the same team with different names?"

Glory drops, not rum

As I stepped out more and more, Cynthia began to speak without interpreters, which gave us much more freedom in Bible studies and small churches. Our fumbles with language led to a humorous incident in a large church of excited believers when I was sharing the vision the Lord had given me. I explained that the power of the Holy Spirit was like drops of God's goodness. I used a Portuguese word that was new to me, and the church began to laugh, though what I was talking about was not funny. After the meeting, I asked the pastor why the people were laughing. Had I said something wrong? He explained that I had said that the drops of glory were like drops of rum being poured out over Brazil. Everyone knew I meant to say, "Like drops of water." He explained that *pingo de aqua* was raindrops. What I had said was *pinga*, which was *rum*. He laughed as he told me, "Listen, brother, they will never forget the sign we are seeing is from Heaven."

Londrina and the Holy Glow

One of the group leaders we befriended wanted to talk with us about one of the churches he was working with that was flowing in the same stream we were in. He asked if we might talk with the pastor and see if we could help him. We agreed and met with the pastor and his family and discerned they were being attacked by a tormenting spirit that could be broken by the power of the Holy Spirit. They were surprised and doubtful, so we had a Bible study that day in God's Word, prayed with and for them, and they opened their hearts to receive the Holy Spirit. The pastor asked us how soon we could preach in their church, and we set a date. The Lord had blessed us with our transportation so we could drive to many of the places we needed to go. This was the Church of Glory, one of our first church contacts in the state of Parana.

As he was telling us about how the church was started and grown, I saw in the Spirit a gorilla hiding behind the couch where they were seated. So, when he finished, I told them about what I saw. Without an explanation, they understood. It was an internal matter in the leadership that was troubling the church and needed attention. Once they dealt with the issue, the Holy Spirit moved powerfully, and many were saved and filled with the Spirit. It was a Holy Ghost explosion. After we left on Monday and drove home, the first phone call we received was the pastor calling to invite us back as soon as possible. He said his people were drunk in the Spirit and could not do anything but praise the Lord and pray. We knew this was something special, and upon our return a week later, the glory of the Lord filled every empty heart with joy and power.

During this time, they invited us to go with them to a prayer meeting on Saturday up in the hills not far from the church. That evening, we drove to a meeting place at the foot of a hill, where the helpers were handing out rug kneeling mats. When we asked what the mats were for, they told us they were to kneel on the ground if we wanted to. After we climbed to the top of a wooded hill, we walked to a clearing that was a circle large enough for maybe twenty people. The place was completely dark. We could not see each other without our cell phone lights. We could barely see the person next to us as we formed a circle and began to sing and worship and praise the Lord. Our singing flowed into prayer and then more worship, and after about thirty minutes, the bark on the trees began to glow with light; then the ground and dead leaves and twigs glowed. The more we prayed, the brighter the glow became, and it went on for about an hour, with prophetic words and prayer for the sick and disabled, the church, the nation, and whatever the Holy Spirit gave us. As we began coming down in our praise and worship, the glow lessened to just a soft light. The word from the pastor was to take our mat and head down the hill. I looked back several times and could see that the only light in the forest was where we had been. After we returned to the home of the people we were staying with, we sat around the kitchen table and asked questions. How long had this been happening? Were there any other places where it happened? When they took some of the dead leaves and twigs home, did they still glow? They told us this had been happening for about a year, and yes, when they had prayer and praise sessions near a container that held the dead leaves and twigs, they would glow. We went back to that place on two more occasions, and we saw the same glow and peace during our praise and worship.

12

Overcoming My Fear

On one of our times at the mission school near the beach, I was asked to work with a team that was assigned to move a diesel generator from a location near the top of a high hill down to the new base camp. Working with two of the students, we loaded the motor and generator on the back of a half-ton pickup truck. The generator and motor must have weighed more than a ton.

Everything went okay until we left the main road, which was paved, and drove onto a dirt road that was unpaved and full of ruts. It had a lot of uneven places and did not have any safety railing.

As we started down the side of the hill, I heard a voice say, "Today you are going to die." I knew that was the voice of the devil. Fear grabbed my heart as I looked over the side of the truck down a drop-off that was about fifty feet straight down. I was sweating, and so were the guys with me who were trying to steady this motor and generator.

Suddenly another voice spoke into my mind. This voice was calm and clear and asked me a question: "Why are you afraid? If you die, you will be with Me, but you are not going to die today. I did not bring you to Brazil to die but to live and preach the Gospel."

After hearing this, I felt a power of boldness, and I spoke out loud to the devil, "You cannot kill me. Fear, get away from me and never return. I am free to do what God has given me to do." The spirit of fear was broken in my life and never returned.

The World Cup rules in Brazil.

Our first trip to Brazil to work with the Mission short term was a time of learning for us. They had the use of a house north of Rio. It was in a location that did not have electrical, gas, or water service so we had to live and learn in this house for a month. We did have an electric generator powered by a diesel motor that we had to prime with gasoline to get it going. We used it to power the lights for evening classes when the sun went down, and it worked great for almost the entire thirty-day period. It was a time when most of the students were taking final exams into the night.

We began to have trouble getting the motor started every day, and the problem was getting worse. One day, a few of the guys helped us load the motor into our pickup truck, and we headed for a town not too far away. We found a shop that sold and repaired the kind of motor we had, and one of their mechanics found the problem, but they could not repair it that day because the World Cup was being played and Brazil was one of the teams playing that day.

We explained our problem and how it was important to get this motor going today. They wanted to know how long the motor had been out of service, and we explained that we had used it the previous night for about three hours. They looked at us and said that could not be true because the injector pump was dead; it could not have run last night. That couldn't have happened. The mechanic said, "Let me hear the whole story." We gave him all the details, and he shook his head and said once again, "Impossible." The shop had the part we needed, so we bought it and asked if we could use their shop to repair it. We repaired it and looked around for a mechanic to help us test it, but the place was empty, so we had to do our own test. The motor worked. While we were still at the repair shop, Brazil scored a goal, and the entire town came alive with gunfire, firecrackers, horns, and shouting. This was something like our Fourth-of-July celebration or Superbowl. Later, the Brazilians explained that when the World Cup is on, especially when Brazil is playing, everything stops.

The World Cup might rule, but our mission school had lights that night at the school house.

Valdo

We met Valdo, one of the many children abandoned on the streets of Rio, when we were working with a church near Copacabana Beach. Our custom was to preach the Word and pray afterward for the people who had needs. He was in line, so we asked him what his need was. Then he explained that his story was too long to tell us there and asked if he could meet with us the following day. We agreed, and the next afternoon, he told us his story.

He was a member of a street gang that roamed the streets of Rio, stealing whatever they could find to eat or wear. Many of the police worked as guards off duty and were hired by local merchants to help protect their stores from these street kids. He was in a group that had been picked up for stealing, taken outside the city, executed, and left for dead. He had been wounded and bleeding and left to die in the woods. After these guys left, he crawled away from that location and found his way to a shelter of vagrants who dressed his wounds and helped him recover.

When he returned to the streets, he was told that the police who had done the execution were being held by the authorities and were awaiting trial or proof that they were guilty. He contacted these investigators and told them his story. He was told that all the boys were killed and left for dead. He was the only one who had information they needed, but they could not protect him from hired assassins who had done similar things while off duty.

When this information was reported internationally, an organization in Italy offered to protect him in their country until his testimony was needed, fly him back to Brazil, and afterward back to Italy. We prayed for the Lord's protection over and around him, that this foreign adoption could take place quickly, and that this type of street crime would come to an end.

Valdo was a street kid, a throw-away child, and a thief, but he was also a diamond God wanted to use to help his country and the world.

In less than a week, the Brazilian document had been provided for him and he was flown to Italy and joined his new family. He did return to Rio under police protection, gave his testimony, and identified the police who had done this. They were prosecuted and sentenced to prison. This type of behavior had been going on for a long time not only in Rio but other cities with homeless kids without any solution until this happened through Valdo. Valdo was a street kid, a throw-away child, and a thief, but he was also a diamond God wanted to use to help his country and the world.

Valdo has written us many times since this happened and thanked us for standing with him, leading him to Christ, and praying for God's protection. He completed his education, graduated from college, and is married with two children. He works for the UN on behalf of street children worldwide.

A Jew and an Arab

We had Bible studies in one of the condos once a week for about a year when it came into my heart that we did not know one another. So I asked the group if we could have a time to hear from each person who had been coming. What kind of work did they do? How had the Bible study helped them?

I did not know at this time that we had a Brazilian who was an Arab from Lebanon and another Brazilian who was a Jew born in Brazil. One of the men stood and

We had an Arab and a Jew in our Bible study—two historic ancient enemies studying about Jesus, the Jewish son of God.

gave his name, his wife's name, and said they had two boys and a girl on the way. He was a merchant, and he added that this was the first time he had been in a meeting like this with a person who was a Jew. A hush came over the room such as I had rarely experienced. We had an Arab and a Jew in our Bible study—two historic ancient enemies studying about Jesus, the Jewish son of God.

This could have been a volatile situation, as the Jewish woman he indicated stood and introduced herself and her family and explained that this was a first for her also and that she had been taught never to trust or have anything to do with Arabs, and they were studying about Jesus together. When she finished, the Arab man stood once again, crossed the room, and stood in front of her. Then he embraced her and added that she was his sister in Christ.

Everyone was speechless, surprised, overjoyed, and shocked at how the Holy Spirit can destroy old hatred and bitterness. The meeting continued with a different atmosphere that evening; many could recognize that we had seen a miracle. Some years later, we had the honor of baptizing our Arab brother and his family in a swimming pool as their Presbyterian pastor looked on. He had asked me if it would be alright if he witnessed this event. We asked him to stay with us as we baptized the entire family one by one in the name of Jesus. I did not know that water immersion baptism was not a part of their belief system. Sometimes it is better to not recognize dogmas and let the Holy Spirit straighten it out.

13

Other Mission Fields

After experiencing success in Brazil, we continued to look for cities or countries where we might sow seed. During our twelve years in Brazil, we received many invitations to come and speak in other countries. My hidden agenda was to see if the Lord wanted to use us in other countries. So, we tested the waters wherever we went—Uruguay, Paraguay, Argentina, Nigeria, Switzerland, England, France, and Russia. It became clear to us that our calling was Brazil. We had so many miracles and divine revelations there, it was clear that the Lord's anointing was on our lives for Brazil.

Argentina on fire

We were invited to speak in Argentina, where we met with a couple who had a Bible study in their home that began a Spirit-filled church in their city. They had belonged to a traditional church for years but felt that there was more to their Christian life than they were experiencing. Their hunger grew as they read the New Testament for themselves and soon prayed according to the passages in the Bible. One evening as they met with friends, they began discussing being Spirit-filled, what it means, and how it occurs. They all began to express joy in a peculiar language that was not Spanish. A sense of joy filled the room where they were, and a Presence guided their thoughts and feelings. Their Bible study went on much longer than usual, but no one wanted to leave that place, and they all knew that something supernatural had happened. But why? It was good, it was refreshing, and they wanted more.

When they finally finished the meeting, they agreed not to tell anyone about what had happened until they could talk with their pastor. The husband of this couple was an executive of a large company in the city, and when he arrived at his office and tried to greet people he met, what came out of his mouth was that language they all had spoken the night before. He hid out in the washroom for the rest of the day, trying to speak in his own language (Spanish) but he could not. When his workday was over, he rushed home to find his wife on her knees crying with her hands lifted and speaking that language. He joined her, and the others who had been there the night before showed up at their home weeping with tears of joy over what was happening.

Later, after a time of praise, their Spanish language returned, and they called the pastor and asked if he could come over to their home and help them with this matter, which he did. After hearing their story, he cautioned them not to tell anyone in their church about this event; this was not of God. They agreed, but after he had given a long theological reason and left their meeting, they continued because they felt that what had happened was the work of the Holy Spirit.

They contacted a Pentecostal pastor, and after asking many questions, he offered to meet with them the next day. They asked him why not tonight, to which he agreed. The moment he stepped into their home, he knew that the Spirit of the Lord was among them, and he explained to them out of the Book of Acts chapter two about the Holy Spirit. After his explanation, the same thing happened, and the power came upon them again, filling them with joy unspeakable. They continued to have their Bible studies, inviting those who wanted more of the presence of the Lord. This grew into a church that had a tremendous impact on the city, producing good Spirit-filled teachers and leaders.

Our permanent visas

For international travel, you must have a passport that identifies you to a country and a visa that shows you are in that foreign country legally for a certain period. After living in Brazil for five years on temporary status, we tried to get our permanent visas. We had received numerous offers from individuals who said they could help us for dollars, but we could see these were scams.

After living in Brazil for five years on temporary status, we tried to get our permanent visas.

While looking for the right pathway, we were invited to speak in Sao Paulo. The invitation came by a recommendation from a person we prayed for in another state who was an attorney who dealt with documentation. We called him and agreed to meet in his office. Following our initial conversation, he wanted to know why we were in Brazil working with Mission Volantes de Cristo. We tried to make our story short, but he wanted details about the length of time we were in the country. When we told him the longer version, he informed us that he would assist us in obtaining our visas. It would take approximately a year.

My next question was how much it would cost us. He said five hundred dollars for each. When I asked him how we might pay for this, I could hardly believe what he said next. "You pay me when I get your visas, not until."

When we asked why our history was important to him, he told us about his family—how his father had become the first Baptist in the neighborhood where they lived, and the persecution they suffered, and the difficulties they went through without turning back to their old beliefs. With tears in his eyes, he said, "Your story touched me. Thank you for answering the call to visit Brazil." A year later we received a letter from his office that our visas had been approved and would be ready for us to pick up soon. When we finally received our passport stamp for permanent status, we contacted him to pay what we had asked, and he told us that it had been paid in full.

14

American Visitors

After working in Rio for several years, it came time for us to take a furlough. Our oldest daughter was in the US Navy, stationed at Norfolk, Virginia, so we attempted to schedule some of our ministry in the US near her.

While we were still in Brazil, we met a man who pastored a church in West Virginia. He gave me his card and asked me to call when we were stateside, so we did and stopped by his church to meet his wife and family. We talked for a while, and he asked me if I could speak in his church on Sunday. I told him I could after I rearranged a few places we were to go. This was one of those God's incidents that happen when you work for the Lord. I asked him to show me where there was an inexpensive motel nearby, but he and his wife would not hear of it. We were their house-guests and would be staying with them for the weekend.

We had a good conversation about church and missions and how we had answered the call to Brazil. As we were visiting, his wife received a call from a family member in another state that a relative had passed away. She told them she would make the necessary arrangements to be there. After she hung up the phone, she told us she had a problem saying goodbye to family or friends after a gathering like a funeral. After everything was over, she would be too stressed out to say goodbye. We asked her a few questions and asked if we could pray for her. When she said yes, we called out a spirit called torment, stress, and anxiety and broke its power over her. We prayed for many in the church, and the next day we moved on to our next destination. We had a great time and made new friends in West Virginia.

About a week before we were to leave for Brazil, this pastor asked me if we could pay them another visit, so we made the arrangements to minister there on our final Sunday. We enjoyed our time with them and their church. During our conversation about our needs, he asked the church if anyone would like to purchase new tires for our van because the Lord had told him and his wife to take us shopping. His wife bought whatever Cynthia wanted, and he bought whatever I wanted or needed—a new suit, tie, socks, shirt, and trench coat. We were blessed as they paid the bill with smiles on their faces. His wife asked us if we remembered the incident of one of her relatives passing away and her confession of anxiety when saying goodbye after a visit with her family or friends. She said this time there had been no torment or stress when it came time to leave. She gave us a big hug and thanked us for hearing from heaven.

Another young woman came forward with a request for prayer. She and her husband were trying to conceive a child and were having no success. The doctors had tried everything they

His wife bought whatever Cynthia wanted, and he bought whatever I wanted or needed.

knew to no avail. We always ask a woman who wants a child if she and her husband agree on how many they want. Once the Lord turns on your ability to reproduce, you might have more children than you want, so we prayed in agreement for what they were asking. The next time we returned to that city, this woman could not wait to tell us she was pregnant with their first child. The joy in her face and eyes told the story.

The Lord opened doors of opportunity for us.
The Lord caused us to be in the right place at the right time to meet with mayors, governmental officials, lawyers, public defenders, prosecutors, diplomats, and parents who love their children and want the best for them.

A couple from Barra, near our apartment, became our biggest and best supporters for our work among the middle class. We were always receiving invitations to meet their acquaintances who held top positions in the city. At one of these lunch meetings, we were introduced to the husband of a woman we had led to the Lord. The wife informed us that they had difficulty in their marriage and asked if we would meet them for lunch in their condo.

The husband confessed he did not believe God was doing everything his wife and daughter were reporting. I could feel the compassion of the Lord for this man, and the Spirit prompted me to ask what it would take for him to believe that the Spirit of God would do everything he had heard. He quickly said that if God touched him right now, he would believe. So we took a step of faith and asked if we could pray for him right now. He agreed and we touched him lightly on the head and prayed. We asked the Holy Spirit to touch him in a manner that he would understand it was from Heaven. The man began to dance, jumping up and down. It was difficult to keep from laughing at seeing this professional businessman dancing in his dining room with a smile on his face. He went on for a while and when he stopped, we could see the tears in his eyes over what had just happened to him. Like many men who did not believe, he tried to hide his hunger for truth and for something that was real. He was filled with joy, and we led him to the Lord and robbed hell of another soul.

We were learning week by week.
We taught others what we were learning about unclean spirit demons, to set the captives free from demonic powers. They openly talked about our work among the poor and gang-infested areas of Rio, where we had an open door to preach the Gospel.

One married couple told us this story about how they dealt with a person who was demon-possessed who came to one of their Bible studies for the workers in their building. We had completed several classes on what the Bible says about demons, but the couple had never seen a manifestation. They told us that the Bible study had begun with Scripture reading and prayer followed by questions. The wife was leading the session, as her husband could not attend that night. As she was answering a question from one of the workers, another worker began to growl and stare with glassy eyes at her, and all those who were near the man began to move away. The woman looked the growling man in the eye and spoke to the demon to stop it and leave right now. The growling stopped, and the man went limp and fell on the floor. When he returned to himself, he asked what had happened, and she asked him if he had ever gone to a spiritist center for any reason. He responded that he had gone once and never again. She explained the danger of visiting those places of darkness and becoming polluted. They prayed for the man and his family and answered more questions before closing the meeting. Afterward, she and her husband laughed and cried about the incident, and he asked her not to do that again, to wait and let Celester or Cynthia take care of it.

We usually asked the pastors in small towns if they had members who were a thorn in their side (problem people), and there were always some. We discovered that some of those people are rough diamonds who can be recovered by the Holy Spirit. The Gospel of Mark reveals a clear picture for the believer of what to do when dealing with demons.

There was one occasion when we were invited to a small town that was being tormented by demonic attacks. There was a woman who had been identified as a good Christian who stopped leaving her house or coming to church. She would accept visitors but would not go outside. The pastor took us to her house and introduced us to her, then left us there. She seated us and offered us coffee, which we accepted and began to talk with her. We asked her why she was no longer going outside or to church, and she had no explanation other than she did not want to. We asked her if we could pray with her. The Holy Spirit gave us revelation that a tormenting spirit had attacked her with fear, and we addressed that attack and broke its power over her and led her in a reconfirmation of her faith in Jesus. We asked her about her family and friends and then invited her to go outside with us. She accepted, and we walked out into the street and then toward the center of the town. She talked and laughed and waved at her neighbors. We could see the attention this event was attracting, so we began to invite people to come to church that evening to witness the power of the Holy Spirit.

15

Healing for the Hurting

We encountered a similar situation in a different town in a traditional church as we were teaching about God's Kingdom and healing of past hurts. We offered to pray for all the leaders and their wives first. A few of the wives were not present, and we continued with prayer for those who had needs. We asked the pastor if we could visit a few of the homes of the leaders' wives who were not at church that night, and he said he would arrange for that.

The next morning as we were talking, I felt in my heart that the Spirit was working on this. We were invited to have lunch at one of the elders' homes, and he would not be there because of his job. His wife had prepared a delicious meal, and afterward, we sat and talked for a while. We had another couple with us whom we were mentoring in this kind of ministry. We asked the woman of the house if we could pray for her, and she said yes.

As we were praying, we could feel an evil presence in her, and we asked her to tell us about her life before she was married. She told us that she was from a family of boys. She was the only girl, and when she was about thirteen, her mother died and she took on the responsibility of cooking, cleaning, and washing. Her father started sleeping with her and sex came next. She thought that this could not be wrong because this was her father. Then her brothers began to have use her sexually until she was about sixteen, when her friends told her this was not right. Later, she met a boy from her town and began dating and later was married to get out of that situation in her home.

Her husband, who was a Christian, led her to the Lord, and they had two children, but she did not love him. She hated all men, especially her father and brothers. She was emotionally lost and physically cold toward her husband and was looking for a way out of this situation.

We explained that what happened to her was wrong and should never have happened. We led her in prayers of forgiveness for her father and brothers and gave it to the Lord. We told her, "Our concern is about you lying to your husband and polluting your children. They had nothing to do with what happened to you, and what is happening in your family is equally wrong. We want to pray with you for forgiveness for what you have done and are doing and allow the Spirit of God to fill your heart with love for your father and his family."

When she did, the Spirit of God did what He does so well—He delivered her from her past. And a sweet smile came over her face with joy. That evening she was at church, and she looked like a new woman, smiling, and hugging her husband and church family. She was rescued from darkness.

The Kingdom and the church

One of our main teachings after a person received salvation was the Kingdom of God and the power of the Holy Spirit to heal and deliver those who had been made captives by false teaching. The Word of God tells us do not be moved by what you see because it is temporary; what you do not see is permanent.

When we returned from one of our trips back to the US, we were anxious to hear from our Bible study group how things had gone in this high-rise meeting place. They told us about one of the teenage girls who lived in this complex who had been hit by a car and was not expected to live because of an uncontrollable hemorrhage in her neck and chin. The people in our Bible study knew her and her parents, and when they got the news many of them met at the nearby clinic where she was taken. The doctor attending to her did not give her much chance to survive because of the massive bleeding.

The doctor attending to her did not give her much chance to survive because of the massive bleeding.

Our group asked if they might go in and see her, and he said no more than three at a time. They all agreed to pray for the Spirit to stop this hemorrhage, and three of them went in and laid hands on her and spoke to the blood to stop and clot in the deep cut in her chin. They tried to give comfort and encourage her to hold on. When the nurse came to usher them out, she saw that the bleeding had stopped. She wanted to know what they had done to her to stop the bleeding. They explained they were Christians and believed what the Bible teaches: to pray and speak to the affliction and trust the Lord, which is what they had done.

The doctor confirmed that the hemorrhage had stopped and bandaged her up, explaining that the wound would heal but she would have to live with an ugly scar on her face. Weeks later, when the doctor removed the bandages, there was not a mark on her face. The medical staff were surprised and joyful at the same time.

Stay free so I can use you wherever you go.
In the beginning of our ministry, the Lord gave us a clear word to not join any denominational group. He guided us away from becoming entangled in any denominational doctrine that would hinder our work to the body of Christ. The Lord used us to mend relations between churches and pastors. We had many discussions with pastors who wanted us to come under their denominational covering. We always declined so we could follow the word we had received from the Lord.

When we had plans to work in a location, we made advance connections with other churches and pastors so they would know we would be in their area and the dates that we were scheduled. If we had a positive response to their request to minister the following week or weekend, we would do that. We had offers from a few well-established churches to come on board and join their denomination and work under their umbrella with a salary, apartment, and car. This was a test of obedience to the word of the Lord, which we obeyed. By this point in time, the ministry had grown enough for us to help other ministers touch many more people in the work of the Lord and get started. We had also trained several translators to work with short-term missionaries.

When we began to grow in Brazil
We had opportunities to start a church, which the Lord had told us not to do. Our main assignment was to preach the Good News, help the established churches do what the Lord had for them to

do, and encourage struggling churches to find a way to fulfill their calling. We knew a time would come for us to return to the US. The Lord had told us this, and when that time came, we prepared as best we could with the team we had trained, to continue to serve in mission-minded churches that needed our help.

Freedom is not free, physically or spiritually. The Spirit of God instructed us to never charge churches or people for what we do, telling us, "I will cause people to give you what you need when you need it." After five years of ministry among various churches in Rio, Espirito Santo, Sao Paulo, and Parana, I saw the power of the Lord to save and deliver all kinds of troubles. The Spirit of the Lord caused churches to give into our ministry in Brazil and the US. It was as if someone had turned on the lights in almost every place we went. This was truly a move of the Spirit on our behalf, and our commitment to go where the Lord opened the door for us produced good fruit for the Kingdom.

There is a process we must go through.
The process is what builds character and stamina to do our best always. This happened to us as we helped churches and those in business or government. The Lord was building in us the ability and ingenuity to help others. There were a few missteps along the way, but the Lord helped us overcome those things that had been sent to destroy us. There were team members we had to break connections with because they could not see or understand what the Spirit was doing through us.

16

Anointing of the Holy Spirit

Over the years, the Spirit has revealed to us the anointing that is on us and with us and how our decision to confess Jesus as our Lord and Savior changed everything for us and our family. It was like moving from a road filled with dark places to a road filled with good places and things. We saw it without having the vocabulary or understanding why.

Our move from Chicago to Anderson was just a first step on the right road. We were being renewed and molded into new creations in Christ. There was not any lightning or thunder, just a revelation to do the right thing—almost like having a Midas touch, without the gold part, but success and seeing things work out in the right way. Things like attending a meeting that was divided or chaotic and when we were asked to give input, answers would suddenly come to mind and bring peace and direction.

On occasion, we were invited to a meeting just to bring clarity, peace, and a clear direction. These events would occur spontaneously, and at the time, it was not clear to us why, but now we can see it was the anointing of the Spirit at work in us and through us. It happened too often for it to be coincidence.

Lack of uprightness

One of the lies from hell is corruption: doing what is evil and calling it good, double-dealing, moral and physical wrongness. We had heard about corruption in the US business and political arena, but what we had seen in our own country was in no way equal to what we saw in Brazil. Lying seemed to be a way of life in many places in Brazil, while seeing and hearing the truth gave us a new respect for what is right. We knew we were called to resist any agreement with words and ways that were not right or true.

We knew we were called to resist any agreement with words and ways that were not right or true.

We were not involved in politics, though we met with many politicians who wanted to use the church for their own purposes. Many times, we had to use caution when asking questions about Brazilian leaders and what they said or did. The Lord made it clear to us that we were not there to change the Brazilian culture or politics. Our work was to change their minds from a worldly nature to Christ's likeness.

The Lord clearly told us, "Do not get involved in corruption in any form. It has become a way of life for many in this country. In civil government, political, or the justice system, the church, and in everyday life, corruption has become acceptable. My people must stand up for what is right, be just and honest, and fight for those things that agree with My Word," says the Lord. "I will be with you. Resist corrupt practices and dishonest dealings wherever you go, whatever you do. Corruption among My people must die by the will of the nation. It is an abomination to Me. Free will is my gift to humanity, a God-given gift to every person. If you choose the evil way, the way of darkness, you reap the fruit of darkness. False dealings, lying, cheating, and crookedness will be your reward. If you choose the path of righteousness, justice, goodness, mercy, truth, and honest judgments shall remain with you."

Holy Spirit is the interpreter.
The Holy Spirit not only guides us, teaches us, strengthens us, gives us wisdom, protects us, and fills us with Himself, He also interprets where we are, where we are going, and what we are doing or not doing. The Spirit was doing this in our lives. As we helped others, He was helping us, raising us in the knowledge and ways of the Lord.

We were not educationally trained in psychology or how to counsel people who are depressed, stressed out, walking in doubt and unbelief, and full of memories of bad decisions, failures, and bad decisions. This was a God-given gift for us to always pray for the needs of the people after the message was preached. This was Godly wisdom at work in us and the place where we were preaching. We always asked that person if we could pray for them and got their permission and then prayed over what they just told us. The Spirit of God gave us an understanding of what he or she had just said and caused us to know what the real problem was—wisdom to know the real problem and follow the leading of the Spirit. We could then continue praying for what He was showing us and how to deal with the situation. He knows the mind and will of God and guided us on how to pray the Lord's solution for their difficulties. Many times, it was so smooth we were unaware that Godly wisdom just spoke. Sometimes, a physical manifestation would reveal to us demonic control or a need for salvation.

After we became familiar with the pastor and the church where we were ministering, we would ask them to allow us to work with their most difficult people. We discovered many people who are diamonds in the flesh covered up by the enemy and his forces. The Lord was using us to uncover and get rid of that wounded place in a person's life. We discovered that many of the pastors were bi-vocational and did not have the time or patience to deal with every problem person in their congregation, and we were God's answer to their prayers.

Christian life is like a puzzle.
Some puzzles have thousands of pieces that fit perfectly in only one place to complete a beautiful picture. Each piece is important, and when we bring them together, they create the likeness of Christ. If pieces are missing, the picture is not complete. We are in Christ, forgiven, washed in His blood, but incomplete without other pieces that join with us. The Spirit caused us to understand that our lives are like that physically, mentally, and emotionally. In life, we all have a place where we fit. The church is like this also. When we talk with someone about their place in their church, they might say that they do not have a place or have not yet found where they fit. But that is usually not true. Our ministry was in place in Brazil to help people find their place in the Kingdom and in the church.

A demon we named suicide
Arriving at our apartment one evening, we met a large group of people standing in the parking lot looking up at something on the upper floors. As we exited our car, a few people ran over to us, shouting, "Pastor, pastor!" They explained that one of the

building's residents was standing in the window outside his apartment threatening to jump and kill himself. "Can you do something to help him? Don't let him do this."

We looked up, raised our hands, pointed our fingers at the man, and in a loud voice commanded the spirit of suicide to let him go. We then went inside and took the elevator to his apartment floor where the hallway was filled with people, some crying, others talking loudly while they made a pathway for us. When we reached the doorway to the apartment, it flew open, and a quietness came over the room. We were led to a bedroom loaded with people shouting at the man and pleading for him not to jump and come out of the window.

We spoke with authority to what we perceived was an evil spirit controlling him. We bound it and commanded it to stop tormenting this man and let him go. He seemed to freeze with a bewildered look on his face. We then entered the room and approached him cautiously. I told him to reach out to me and give me his hand, which he did, and we helped him back into the room as he began to weep.

We found out later that he had done a few stupid things with finances that would affect his family. His wife came and stood with him and walked him into a bedroom where he could dress and receive counseling. His wife and friends thanked us for being available to help them, and after that night we began to receive respect from our neighbors in our building.

Divine intervention

During our preparations and travels, we had many challenges that helped us see the hand of God guiding our footsteps and making a way where there was no way.

During our twelve years of living in Brazil and forty years of ministry in other countries, including our own, we have seen the Spirit of God do mighty things that only God could do. The following is just a small list:

- protecting us all the time we lived in and worked in Brazil, Paraguay, Argentina, England, Switzerland, France, Italy, Israel, Russia, Nigeria, and Haiti;
- healing and delivering us from sickness and the debt of over $100,000 from four surgeries for intestinal problems;
- providing the funds for returning to Brazil for follow-ups to our original mission;
- providing four automobiles for us to get to the hard-to-reach places in Brazil;
- providing places to rest when we needed to at no cost to us;
- protecting us from storms and from a bridge washout that would strand us for many days on the side of a mountain on the only road in or out to a town that needed our help.

17

Humble Yourself

We were invited to a group meeting to help resolve differences that were causing problems within the leadership. After three of the leaders had spoken, I was invited to give a word on the problem at hand. I quoted from John 13, where Jesus spoke to His disciples and began to wash and dry their feet. By doing so, He showed His servant heart and humility to serve others and not to be served. God raises up those he chooses to become leaders and places them into positions to lead others. I challenged them to follow this example and wash one other's feet while confessing their love and submission to one another. Men with men and women with women, we witnessed tears of forgiveness as the Spirit touched their hearts. Obedience and humility are two of the Bible precepts that are super important in our lives.

Chosen for this

After five years of working with different churches, we became aware that we were chosen by the Lord to address a ministry that needed to be done. This involved encouraging Brazilian pastors and leaders to become doers of the written Word, not in a legalistic way, but to do what God has said in His Word: preach and teach the Word; raise disciples who would carry forward the Word in the power of the Holy Spirit; and welcome into their churches those who were hungry for the manifestation of God's plan and purpose for His church.

Whenever we made a return trip to the church where we had worked before, we looked for growth and change. It was working, yes, but was it the kind of work we were called to do? Seeing the church growing up, reaching out to the lost, hurting, and confused—for us, that was where the power of the Gospel was most effective. We were chosen to fulfill the truth of God's Word. What a challenge! Did we always carry out the goals we had set for ourselves? No, we had failures and disappointments that taught us valuable lessons for the next time. But we had so many wonderful victories of souls being saved, marriages restored, and young people rescued from drugs and perversion.

Many times, the attack of the enemy was more than we could bear alone, and the power of the Spirit would prevail over our weaknesses. And when we saw impossible barriers crushed, doors opened, and lies exposed, it caused us to see and understand the plan of the Lord. When churches asked us to come and help them resolve problems in their ministry, we felt honored and humbled to be given such a task. And the Spirit of the Lord gave us what we needed for every situation when we needed it.

God can multiply money.

We discovered that when we have been a good steward, supervisor, and manager of the Lord's money, He will pour out His blessing financially. This happened to us when we went to a meeting in Rio where we met two Americans who wanted to see Sugar Loaf and the Christ statue before returning to the US. We were free that day, so we took them to both locations before dropping them at their hotel that evening. They thanked us for taking time out of our day and gave us a just-in-time offering for our ministry. On our way home, we counted the gift, which was one hundred dollars, and we were thankful. We stopped to make a few purchases and then went to another store before arriving home. We were preparing for a trip, so we made another stop before leaving for another city. I asked Cynthia how much we had left, and when she counted the money, it was one hundred dollars. I asked her to count it again, which she did, and she had one hundred dollars. I told her to stop joking, and she said again, "One hundred dollars." I found a place to pull off the road and we both counted one hundred dollars. We began to laugh and cry and shout and came to the realization that the Lord was multiplying what we had and needed without our asking.

That continued for the rest of our trip home. When we bought fuel and paid cash, we had the same amount. No lightning or thunder. The amount we had stayed the same—one hundred dollars—all that day! Glory to the Lord! Every promise of God has a process connected to it. "I'm in you and you are in Me. What you do causes Me to be a part of what you are doing. We are joined together in the Spirit." "You will know for yourselves that I am in My Father, and you are in Me, and I am in you." (John 14:20 AMP).

18

Spiritism and the Graveyard

One part of our training in missiology was understanding spiritism—the images, sacrifices, animals, and people. Spiritism is a relatively new belief system that was brought to Brazil from Europe in the second half of the nineteenth century. It involves the practice of using mediums to contact the dead on behalf of the living as well as reincarnation and consulting spirits for advice and to seek healing. It is definitely not consistent with Christianity. Umbanda is another religion widely practiced in Brazil; it mixes parts of spiritism, some loose elements of Christianity and paganism, intermingled with other forms of idolatry. Contemporary names for both spiritism and Umbanda are witchcraft, voodoo, black magic, and white magic. Rio and Bahia are strongholds of spiritism meeting centers and hundreds of shops that sell all the elements of the practice.

For Cynthia and me, it was an eye-opener to a different kind of demonic worship and a battle that has already been won by Jesus on the Cross and His resurrection from the dead. The main part of our teaching was how to recognize who and what the people who practice spiritism believe. One of our classes was a visit to one of the large graveyards in Rio. As we ministered, we were instructed to look and learn, not to pray, cry, or laugh. We unloaded the class on a side street and walked to the front or entryway where the Umbanda had set up their locations. We saw sacrifices that were scary, bloody, funny, and sad.

Then suddenly, they began to collect their things and load up boxes with their tools in cars and leave. Our leader knew what was happening, and we went to our transportation for the trip back to Seropedica. Our leader got everyone's attention and asked who was praying. His wife raised her hand and confessed that she had never seen anything like what they did in her life. So, she prayed asking the Lord for peace and safety. We all began to laugh about how one frightened, petite Christian woman could shut down the devil's party with prayer.

The enemy sets traps.
We learned that when the Spirit is moving in your ministry, envy and jealousy move also and can begin to manifest without an invitation. Our desire as we ministered in Brazil was to help Christians discover what was God's will for their lives and how they could begin to do whatever that was. We believe that our enemy can see which way we are heading and sets traps to trip us up or block our forward movement to the will of God. As we prayed and listened to the leading of the Spirit, the enemy would move in ways we had never seen or heard and cause us to question the Spirit. We continued to ask for discernment and clarity and fight doubt and unbelief that invaded our thoughts. We soon learned to confess 1 Corinthians 2:16: "But we have the mind of Christ." Not *could have* or *would have* but in the present tense, *we have the mind of Christ*. We had to confess that He was

functioning in us, listen, and obey. The enemy attempts to confuse our trust in the Lord.

We started with translators.

While working in Brazil we started out using translators for our preaching and Bible studies, which helped us get started in speaking to as many as possible in the city. But when we traveled to small faraway places and towns, there were few or sometimes not any translators available, which showed us that we had to learn Portuguese if we were going to speak in rural places. We eventually enrolled in a language school to learn how to communicate in their language.

The other problem was in counseling where matters had to be kept private, especially for pastors and church leaders. We needed to converse privately with individuals, without the intervention of an interpreter. Every believer has a history before accepting Christ and although we understand this, many churches are still working under legalism and old doctrines.

> *We needed to converse privately with individuals, without the intervention of an interpreter.*

A few years into our journey I asked the Lord to let us go home. I told Him, "You have called the wrong person for this mission." I was having a real problem learning Portuguese, and I didn't feel I was connecting with the Lord during my prayer time. If He had someone else He wanted to use, I was ready to return to the US. After a few days I heard the voice of the Lord say I could go home if I wanted to, but first He wanted me to read the story about the children of Israel crossing the desert to the Promised Land. When I read again of how the Lord fed them with manna from heaven, water to drink from the rocks, none of their enemies could defeat them, their clothes did not wear out, I confessed I wanted to stay in Brazil and finish the assignment He had given us.

Even after language school, I was having problems speaking and writing. The Spirit told me to watch the evening news programs on TV. I did not understand why, but I watched and paid close attention to the reporters' words coming out of their mouths, the expressions they used, how they formed the Portuguese guttural and nasal sounds, and I repeated what I heard them say. Slowly, I could imitate them and say the words from the Bible, and regular conversation started flowing out of my mouth.

Even after language school, I was having problems speaking and writing.

I also asked people I knew if they could understand what I was saying. I found out from many of the Brazilians that my efforts meant more than just words and correctness to them.

Anointing of the Spirit

The anointing was getting stronger on our ministry, and the battles kept coming, but so did the victories. Doors opened to us, and we learned to do what the Lord was doing. As we study the Scriptures, we see how the Lord modeled many of the historical stories for our benefit of what to do and not do. The Old Testament is filled with accounts of what happened to the people involved and how it affected their families and the next generation. I call these modeling, stories filled with details of before and after a lesson.

It became clear to us that the Lord, Creator of the universe and humanity, has modeled for all humanity to see what He desires of us in our journey in this life. He has said it, modeled it, and given examples on all sides of what we should do. Our problem is not being able to recognize the message given. The more I read the Old Testament, the more I can see the examples and warnings laid before us to guide our footsteps as we go forward.

Working with others

During our ministry in Curitiba, we met foreign missionaries who specialized in agriculture and trained in small towns. We cross-trained with them because they were interested in the spiritual side of mission work, an area where the Lord blessed us with success. At times, we shared stories about places that were open to us and warned them about areas of danger in the rural areas that were still jungle to us.

We were introduced to small churches that were experiencing difficulties confronting spiritism. A few of these pastors invited us to minister in their Bible studies with new believers. One of these was a church on a large island in a river that could only be reached by boat. At one of these meetings, storm clouds began to form with high winds. Earlier, there had been no wind, and the sky was blue with no clouds. We were praying for the sick and other needs when our host warned us to get to the boats before the storm hit or we would be stranded on the island until the water receded, which could be two or more days. We felt in the Spirit that this was an attack from the enemy, so we lifted our hands to the clouds and commanded the rain to not fall in the area where we were. The people there looked at us as if we had sprouted horns, and then we returned to our ministry to the people. As the wind began to die down, the people began to lift their hands to heaven in prayer to thank the Lord for stopping the wind and rain. On our way back to the mainland, the leader asked if we could return for more of this kind of teaching and ministry. Our host promised to send a team to continue working with them because this stop was not on our agenda.

Passports and piranhas in Paraguay

For a short season, we lived in Paraguay with a pastor friend until our visas could be renewed. There was a military coup in Paraguay while we were there. The borders were closed, and we couldn't leave Paraguay to return to Brazil.

While we were waiting, our friends invited us to a picnic. This gave us more time with them, so we accepted. That morning, the Lord impressed on my heart to take our passports with us. I tried to protest, but He pressed His will more, so I put them in my pocket in obedience.

As we were having a good time and enjoying the food, one of the local men in the group asked if we had tried to fish in their river. "Let me show you," he offered. The man prepared a pole and a float, put the bait on the hook, and explained how to put it into the water. As soon as the bait sank in the water, a lot of ripples circled around Cynthia's float, which quickly disappeared under the water.

My wife had never fished, so when the line went tight, she began to scream and shout and dance as they helped her pull the fish onto the shore. One of the guys grabbed a small club and hit the fish's head to still it. Then he swiftly cut off its head. They asked if we knew what kind of fish it was, and we shook our heads no. He then picked up the head and squeezed it until its mouth opened and we could see the jagged sharp teeth.

I asked what kind of fish that was, and they explained that it was a piranha, and it was very dangerous. Cynthia had never caught a fish in the US, and here in Paraguay she caught one of the most dangerous fish in the world.

The Paraguayans were laughing because they knew the stream had piranha fish in it, and when they showed us the mouth and teeth, we knew this was not just an ordinary fish. That's when they told us about the piranhas and that this stream had them. We could see how much laughter the local people could get when they made a joke on Americans.

The locals told us a fish story about a Brazilian farmer who blocked off part of a river near his home. He knew the river had piranhas. The farmer pushed a sick cow with cuts on its body into the water, where it was quickly ripped apart to a skeleton by a school of hungry piranhas.

Miracle of the passports
One of the Brazilian missionaries we had met several years earlier was also at the picnic. He asked why we were in Paraguay. When we explained our visa problem, he asked if I had our passports with me. I quickly produced them and passed them to him. After a few minutes, he asked if we could meet him the next morning at the Brazilian consulate. He explained that the person in charge could straighten this out for us.

We did as he asked and met him at the consulate. He took our passports, disappeared for about half an hour, and returned with the necessary forms for us to fill out and pay the processing fee to a local bank for the passports to be stamped. Then he disappeared again. When he reappeared, he had two receipts for our passports for the next day. The borders reopened, and we were able to return to Brazil without further delay.

19

We Did Not Know

We never knew how many people were changed by our ministry in the places the Lord sent us. We still try to go back as often as we can to see what the Lord has done.

We learned a song that touched our hearts, and we began using it wherever we ministered. From where and by whom I do not know, but we sang it in English and in Portuguese, and it became our opening music for our meetings. The words are "In His presence, there is joy and peace. I will linger and stay in His presence day by day till His likeness be revealed in me." This song became a part of what the Lord was doing in many cities and churches.

We realized we are living letters, living stones. "To whom coming, as unto a living stone, disallowed indeed of men, but chosen of God, and precious, Ye also, as lively stones, are built up a spiritual house, an holy priesthood, to offer up spiritual sacrifices, acceptable to God by Jesus Christ" (1 Peter 2:4-5 KJV).

Our three daughters have benefited from what the Spirit did through us in the US and other countries of the world. They followed and obeyed the leading of the Spirit as He led us in the Word.

"For the promise is to you and your children, and to all who are afar off, as many as the Lord our God will call" (Acts 2:39 NKJV).

A case of mistaken identity

Two years after we moved back to the US, I received a notice from the Brazilian government that I should appear in person to answer questions concerning my responsibility as a citizen of Brazil. I contacted friends of ours to investigate the matter for me. They informed me that it was legitimate and that I should answer and appear in person as soon as possible, so I did. I took all my documents with me to prove I was an American citizen and that my wife and I had lived and worked for a while in Brazil on permanent visas.

The department of the Brazilian government would be equivalent to our Social Security Administration here in the United States. My passport was confiscated, and I was assigned to the agent who was doing the investigation. He explained that the law governing Brazilian citizens states that if you do not vote in local and federal elections, you lose all benefits under their system. I gave him copies of all my documents, and then his interrogation began with simple questions like where I lived while in Brazil, did I have proof of payment of light bills, gas, and rent, etc. After about an hour of questions to which everything agreed, my passport was returned to me with a "sorry for the mix-up and thank you."

Fighting the forces of darkness

One of the suburbs of Rio had grown large enough to become a self-governing city and was on the ballot for approval for the third time. But because of corruption it never had enough votes for approval. A team oversaw the counting of the votes and knew that

116

the same forces were at work again, so they asked for our help. They explained that we could not have anything to do with the voting because we were not Brazilians. What they wanted us to do was walk around and keep an eye on anyone who was doing anything suspicious, noting what and where. This turned out to be a long day, as we were watching the ones who were watching us. When the votes were counted, the measure passed by a wide margin.

We had talked about the power of the Holy Spirit to defeat the powers of darkness in spiritual and natural matters. Many churches had been invited to join in prayer for this measure to pass. As we rode home that evening, our friends at the polls told us our presence had stirred up a lot of questions from the polling workers about who we were, what we were doing, and why we were there. They thanked us for being available for this important measure to succeed. This was another sign that we were in the right place at the right time for the right reason.

Some may suggest this was a coincidence, but we do not believe that. When the powers of darkness are at work, the body of Christ can and should intervene. We have witnessed so many divine interventions, there is no room for coincidences. For more than forty years, in many countries, cities, and churches, we have seen divine intervention from heaven flowing according to the will of God.

20

From Rio to the World

Doors to other countries began to open to us. We had already ministered the Word in Uruguay, Paraguay, and Argentina. But when the doors to Europe opened for us to England, France, Switzerland, and Italy, we were blessed with the opportunity to branch out even farther.

This all began with an invitation to a wedding in England for the son of a Canadian couple with whom we were very close. His parents were missionaries living in Brazil who worked with leaders from several countries in Latin America. We had become friends and agreed to lead and oversee a group of Bible school students from England. Their son was completing his advanced studies in theology and missiology.

Cynthia and I contacted three churches that would allow these students to minister in whatever way the Lord would lead them. We laid out the plans for our travel with the group to various cities over two weeks. We met with them and explained what we would be doing, the basic plan during their time with us, and the rules of conduct while they were on this crusade. Cynthia and I wanted to meet with each one of them privately about why they had chosen missionary work as their field of study. A husband-and-wife team came with them as chaperones and oversaw their progress for the school.

Each one of the students was assigned a time when they would give the message that night and the ministry following. As we gave them this assignment, we could see fear set in. As we dealt with their fears and doubts, we discerned that a few of them had been delivered from the streets of their home country, had doubtful conversions to Christ, and traumatic life experiences. Thank God for the Holy Spirit, who turned on the gifts of the Spirit as they were needed to get them free from their past. In two weeks, we saw doubts and fears go away and faith grow in their hearts and minds as they learned to trust the leading of the Spirit and the Word of God to work in their lives. We tried to convince them that this was a journey, not a test from the Lord.

They received a crash course in mission work they will never forget. In this group, we interacted with men and women from England, France, the Philippines, India, and Canada. From this first encounter, we received the opportunity to minister in Switzerland, Italy, and France. We learned that many Christians are being tormented by demon forces, fears, and spiritual blindness. Before the students returned to England, we had a get-together in Rio to say goodbye and to hear from each of them how this part of their journey helped them. They all agreed that they saw and did in Brazil what they could never have done in a classroom in London.

21

England, Switzerland, and France

Doors opened for us to minister in London and Paris. We had enough time in our ministry plans, so we began planning how this trip was going to stretch our budget, mainly the flights to London and back to Brazil. We had already learned to give our requests to the Lord and let the Spirit work. It came to us that we had set aside time to return to the US, so why not combine these trips and check the cost of both before returning to Brazil?

The other invitation was to France to minister during a weekend, working with a ministry to immigrants from the Indian Ocean countries. Many were saved and filled with the Spirit and delivered from the demonic powers of darkness. One of the leaders of that student group was getting married in London and invited us to attend. We contacted a local travel agent about our plans, and after his calculations, we could see this cost was way over our heads, so we asked the Lord to work this out for us. As the time for us to leave drew near, our airline agent gave us a call about a special travel ticket from Brazil to London to the US and back to Brazil. The ticket was good for thirty days of unlimited flights. We could hardly believe what he was telling us, and all of this for the same price of a passage to the US! We knew this could work, so we booked that flight and started packing. We explained our plans to our Canadian friends and had a time of prayer and rejoicing over what the Lord had opened to us. The next blessing was that we did not need a visa for England, Switzerland, or France, just our passports.

The Lord paid the way.

Our friends from Canada had friends in London who offered us a room in their home for as long as we needed, so we stayed for the wedding and sightseeing in London. We had a little time on our hands before going to Paris, so we asked if they knew of a travel agent who might show us what was available for flights to Switzerland. They did and offered to drop us off at the location that was near.

While we looked at what was available and the cost of each plan, our friend returned to the agency office and listened for a while then stopped by the agent's desk and politely said, "Whatever they choose, I will pay for half the cost." Then she laid her credit card on his desk and left. The three of us were awestruck, flabbergasted, and blown away. She returned in just a few minutes and told us to make sure the package had hotel accommodations. We made our choice and planned for the following day's departure. Our friend returned smiling, checked the details, and collected our tickets. We walked down the street for a short distance and watched the changing of the guards in front of Windsor Castle—what a sight!

Our host asked if we could have a stopover to visit a friend who was ill and not expected to live much longer. We agreed and had a good meeting with the couple. The husband had terminal cancer. We could see that they needed to be encouraged, and we planted a seed of hope in their hearts. When the ladies left for the washroom, I had a chance to talk to the husband one-on-one. I prayed with him after asking him if he was sure of his salvation and spoke life, healing, and recovery to him.

When the ladies returned, the Lord gave me a word for his wife to stop seeing her husband dead in a casket rather than healed and recovered, which was a sign of weak faith in the miracle-working power of the Spirit. Our faith says he's healed, and doubt says he's dying. We all joined hands for a time of prayer, and as we pulled out of their driveway, that man was standing with his wife on their front porch waving as we drove off. Our host told us that he had been bedridden for weeks and seeing him standing and waving goodbye was a miracle.

The next morning at breakfast they thanked us for going with them and encouraging them not to give up and to continue to trust the Lord. They drove us to the airport and told us we were always welcome in their home, and they felt honored to help in any way they could.

Switzerland and miracles

Landing in Zurich, Switzerland, we found that all we needed was our passport to travel anywhere in Europe. We checked into our hotel and asked them to help us with a phone call to our daughter's mother-in-law, who had been a financial supporter of our work in Brazil. She lived in Switzerland and had planned for our visit with her later that day. She gave us detailed instructions on what trains to catch and the station where we should get off. We made our connections with ease and met up with her and her friends in a home for retired church workers. We were asked to speak at their Bible study, and they had questions for us about our mission in Brazil.

You may be asking about this Switzerland connection. How did that happen? Our middle daughter attended Indiana University at Bloomington where she met her husband-to-be after a few years of dating. They were married after graduation, and a few years later, they spent one year meeting his family and living and working in Zurich before returning to Chicago and buying a home. When we told them we were heading to England, they asked us to pay a visit to his mother in Zurich, so we did.

The travel package we paid for was for seven days, so we looked at the map of Europe and asked about trains to Rome, Italy. If we left that evening, we could be in Rome the following morning. The cost was forty dollars each, the same for the return trip. We had four days more before returning to England, so we began to make plans. We packed a small overnight bag, bought our tickets, and caught our train to Rome. The coach cars were comfortable, with four seats facing each other. Our coach filled quickly, and the other passengers began talking with each other—some in Italian, others in French, and still others in Swiss German. So, I asked if anyone spoke English, and they all shook their heads no. I thought maybe someone spoke Portuguese. I asked them in Portuguese if anyone spoke Portuguese, and almost everyone responded and wanted to talk to us, thinking we were Brazilians.

22

Zurich to Rome

The next morning, we were at the train station in Rome. Understanding the Italian language was much easier because Italian, Spanish, Portuguese, and French are all rooted in Latin.

On the main street in the historic portion of the city, we located a currency exchange. While we were standing in line, I saw a man and a woman in front of us with a Chicago tag on their luggage, so I asked in English about the city and questions about exchange rates and where we could find a good hotel for a hot shower. They gave us good directions, and at the check-in counter, I saw a sign advertising bus tours of the city and all the historic sites with the cost and time of departure. I signed up, paid the fare, and went to our room for a hot shower and a change of clothes.

We had a delicious meal before finding our bus for the tour of the city. We kept pinching ourselves as the guide gave us the history of ancient Rome, the Vatican, and all the sights we passed and what happened in each location.

There were only six people on our bus for English-speaking tourists, so we had a private tour, and this is where we met a couple from New Zealand who were retiring without a clue what to do next. We listened to them tell us about their Christian journey, and as they were talking, the Spirit quickened us to pray for them, which we did. The Lord spoke into their lives with such clarity that we knew He was speaking into their hearts.

We spent the entire day seeing what we could, thanking the Lord for this opportunity to minister in Rome. We were from Robbins, Illinois, and here we were in Rome, Italy. This was a dream come true. Our train to Zurich would be leaving at eight o' clock, which gave us enough time to stop by the hotel to collect our things and make our way to the train station with time to spare. We arrived in Zurich the next morning, went back to our hotel, had breakfast, and slept all day.

We were from Robbins, Illinois, and here we were in Rome, Italy.

After our return to Switzerland, we caught our flight back to England and a taxi to the ferryboat to cross the Channel to France. We docked on the other side of the English Channel and caught a train to Paris to meet with our friends for a few days. On our train trip, we met two other Americans and exchanged stories of why we were in France and celebrated Labor Day over a chocolate Easter bunny my wife had in her travel bag.

In Paris, we met with our friends and listened to how much they learned on their trip to Brazil with us and dug into what the Bible school taught those students going into foreign mission ministry. They took us to see the tourist attractions of Paris.

On Sunday we ministered in a closed tavern where many hungry believers were waiting to hear the Word of God. The power of the Spirit was flowing strong, and many were slain in the Spirit and ended up on the floor, speaking in tongues. The Holy Spirit moved powerfully on the mostly Indian and Asian congregation.

After our time in Paris, we boarded a flight to Chicago and then went to Niagara Falls and Norfolk, Virginia, spending time in each one of these cities with relatives and churches that supported our work in Brazil. Then we attended our high school class reunion and took our final flight from Virginia to Rio, Brazil. We did all that traveling in one month on our special ticket package.

That was the beginning of our involvement in missions in other countries, submitting ourselves to the direction of the Spirit of the Lord. Every place we went, every person we met, the Lord would give us a word, a direction, a picture for that person or couple. If the picture was in color, it was now or for the future; if the picture was gray or dark, it was something connected to the past. When I asked the Lord what the meaning was or to give me understanding, we received more spontaneous revelations than ever before. We became comfortable with what the Lord was showing us, and when we talked to the person later, they would confirm the meaning.

23

Prison Doors Open to Us

We were introduced to two English-speaking foreign ex-prisoners who were trying to help other foreigners imprisoned in Brazilian jails. The one we befriended was Gary, who spoke to us about the difficulty foreigners had in Brazilian jails. We listened to his story of how he was incarcerated for drug possession in Peru, which is usually fifteen years or dismissed if you pay the fine under the table.

He had served a few years of his sentence and came to accept Jesus and began evangelizing the prison and was paroled to the streets of the capital city of Peru. He and his German buddy decided to cross the border into Brazil. He put together a story about losing his passport for England's consulate in Rio, in hopes of getting a replacement to get back to England. He explained how he had accepted the Lord in prison and wanted to work with people incarcerated on drug charges and those who needed help. He was given a temporary passport until they could work on his case. I heard the Lord tell us to help him and mentor him. So, Gary became the first foreign disciple we took on under the leadership of the Lord. He was a rough diamond the Lord wanted us to work with to help those who needed help in Brazil, Uruguay, and Paraguay prison systems.

Bible study stirred up the devil.

We had begun a Bible study class in a language school for the director and teachers not attached to a church or Christian-based group. We invited Gary and his girlfriend to join us weekly for this group that was growing in numbers and understanding. We were teaching the group about spiritism, witchcraft, demons, and deliverance when a demon manifested in Gary and began to shout, "I want out of here." He jumped up and ran to the door and kicked the door, saying over and over, "Let me out!"

Now mind you, this was a business in operation that was having classes in the upper rooms, and in this downstairs conference room was a man with a demon manifesting with noise and violent action. I ran to him, got in his face, and shouted, "Stop! Shut up and come out now!" Cynthia and I had seen this before in some of the churches, but this was a first in a public business. Those who were there were shocked and even terrified. Gary's eyes were glassy, his face was contorted, and he looked dangerous. I got him under control, looked him in the eye to make sure he was tuned in, and told him we would meet with him later to talk.

The following day, I dug into his background and prison experience and discovered that he had a ton of bad experiences in life and imprisonment, no connection with church, the Bible, or anything Christian-based or voodoo, spiritism, or witchcraft. Gary had the strong personality of a leader. In prison, he had to defend himself and got into a few fights for survival and food. He had witnessed many murders. We took him through deliverance from evil forces and commanded every unclean spirit to loose him. We led him in prayer and confession of Christ as his Savior and Lord. From that day forward, he was free from demonic control, and he began to read his Bible and grow in the work of the Lord.

24

Gary, a Minister of the Lord

Gary was given the gift of hearing the cries and agony of those behind bars. Gary and I were going somewhere by bus in Rio, in the middle of a conversation, when he began to weep for no clear reason. I asked him what was wrong, and he told me we were near a jail or prison because he could hear their cries for help. I looked at him in disbelief over what he was saying. He said, "Let's get off, and I can show you." So we did, and we began to walk in the direction to which he pointed.

We asked a person on the street if there was a prison near the location where we were standing. The person gestured in the direction we were walking, and we soon came to a sign that pointed toward where we were heading and the name of the prison. I asked Gary if he knew this name or the prison, and he told me he did not. The closer we approached, the faster he walked because the cries were getting louder. We arrived at a place with high walls, guard towers, and an entrance with a guard. We asked if this was a prison and if they let visitors meet and talk to prisoners. The guard told us we would need to go to the office and fill out a visitor card with the name of our church or organization, and

Saturday was the only day for visitors. We did what he had asked and received our passes for visitation. Gary went alone on Saturday because I was already committed to another event and could not go with him. He told me about his visit on Saturday, that there were two Americans who wanted to visit and help those who needed help. He told me he believed that the Spirit gave him this sensitivity because of his time of being incarcerated.

This happened two more times while I was with him in Uruguay and Paraguay. He told me about the Brits and Americans who had critical medical needs the prison system could not afford to pay for. He took it upon himself and contacted their families for help.

Chuck Colson's prison ministry invited him to speak at their regional conference held in Brazil.

25

Nigeria

I was invited to work with two other pastors among the Yoruba tribe in Nigeria, Africa. Our goal for this mission was to encourage churches in the capital city and several towns. We arrived at the international airport in the capital city, and the authorities guided us through the passport and baggage inspection to our host who was waiting for us. After we reached the place that would be used for our base, we had a meal and time to rest before the evening's ministry. They had prepared a team of helpers to assist with the languages and customs for our time with them. We were informed that we would be ministering in places that had different languages and customs. The place where we were staying was a mission training school, and it would be our base for our time with them during our rest and preparation for ministry to the hungry hearts of the people. In each location was a different tribe with its king, and we spent time with him first before we spoke to the people.

I asked all of them about tribal beliefs. Every tribe we met confessed Christ as their Savior. I ask them about spiritism that had been passed along from their ancestors. They were curious about my knowledge of idols and beliefs they no longer practiced. I told them about our ministry in Brazil and that many Brazilians were descendants from Africa and still practiced spiritism, voodoo, and witchcraft. We had a good exchange and a powerful ministry of deliverance for those who still lived under family curses and spiritual attacks without understanding why. We ministered from the Word of God that in some of these situations they were being attacked even after they had accepted Jesus as Lord in their life. We taught how the Bible reveals that we are spirit, soul, and body. Each one of us is a spiritual being, which we receive at conception, that gives us a God awareness. We have a soul that gives us self-awareness—I am alive, I can feel, think, create, like, love, laugh, cry—our mind, will, and emotions. I live in a body, a physical house that gives me world awareness. I am aware of the world I live in. It's hot, it's cold, it's windy, it's sunny or dark. Many of them had never heard a teaching like this before, and it helped some of them to see why we need the Word of God every day in our lives.

Near the end of our time with the churches, the other pastors asked me if I would speak to this large church about anything the Lord had revealed to me while here in their country. I did, and first off, I thanked them for allowing us to minister what the Lord had laid on our hearts. I followed this with a question: "How many of you have a mark, tattoo, cut, or brand on your body that identifies you with a certain tribe?" Almost every person in the church raised their hand. I told them that I was the son of an African family stolen from Africa hundreds of years ago and enslaved in America.

"And here I am today, hundreds of years later, a son of Africa with African blood from my ancestors. And I see all these hands raised to let me know you are from different tribes in this great nation. What I see is Africans tall and short, small and large, dark and not so dark, but all of you are Africans from Nigeria. From different tribes, but Africans; from different mothers and fathers, yet Africans. The only reason I can see that the slave trade flourished was because of tribalism. One tribe over another helped to enslave African people years ago. The same conditions that existed hundreds of years ago remain today, separating one tribe from another due to tribal beliefs or differences. My prayer is that the leaders of your tribes would see that division is not the solution to Nigeria's problems, but that God has a better way for the good of all Africans."

I asked them to join me in prayer to seek God's help in this goal. We all prayed together as one for the will of God to prevail over Africa. After the meeting, we prayed for the needs of the people. The pastor came to me and thanked me for this message which his people and all Africans needed to hear. That message needed to come from an African outside of Africa. He told me if he gave that message in his church, it would be empty the following Sunday.

It had always been a desire in my heart to visit Africa, but the opportunity to do so had never opened, so I placed it on the back burner and thought it would never happen. On that day in Nigeria, Africa, I was speaking to an all-African congregation in a church about what the Lord had revealed to me about tribalism and division that was hurting Africa. An African American born and raised in Robbins, Illinois, gave that important message that day.

26

Israel

Our trip to Israel was a desire of our heart. I happened to be looking at a TV news report one evening when an advertisement about visiting Israel came on. As I watched the presentation, I heard the Spirit say, "This door is opened to you." I began thinking about the cost and time when I heard these words: "If not now, when?" I asked my wife, "Is this one of those things you would like to do?" Without any hesitation, she said, "Yes, let's do it."

We contacted the organization, paid for the registration, and embarked on the trip of a lifetime. Our trip began with the Holy Spirit giving us a divine encounter in the New Jersey airport, where we gathered for departure from the US. We met a man in a wheelchair who was going on the same trip to Israel. We talked with him for a while and listened to his story. The longer we ministered, the more we learned that everyone has a story—good, bad, or ugly—everyone has something that has marked them, sometimes from childhood, for the rest of their life. This man had been diagnosed with terminal cancer and had been advised to do whatever he was going to do because he did not have much time left. We prayed for him and told him to have faith in the promises of God about life and death. "When your life comes to an end, accept it with peace."

We did not see him again until we were halfway to Tel Aviv. We talked with one of the flight attendants, and she told us he was a real problem for her. When she pointed him out, we told her we would talk to him. He remembered us from the airport. As we dug into what was bothering him, the Spirit revealed that a spirit was tormenting him. We had learned that when the Spirit of God reveals this kind of torment, we should offer to pray for deliverance ASAP. He said he wanted to be free of this torment, so we laid hands on him and commanded the tormenting spirit to leave him now and for the peace of the Lord to rest upon him. We could see that he began to relax and even smile, and we told him to call us if he had any more trouble, please let us know.

In Jerusalem

The Jewish markets were closed on Saturday, and the Arabs were open, so we made some of our purchases from the Arab vendors. We found a store that sold T-shirts, and as the merchant showed us what he had, we could see that he had injured his right arm, so we asked him about it. He told us his story about being caught in a machine when he was young. The doctors told him he would live with this injury for the rest of his life. So, we asked him if we could pray for him. He replied, I'm a Palestinian Muslim." We looked him in the eye and told him there was only one God in the whole world with many names and He fixes conditions like this. With his permission, we laid hands on him and prayed for the Lord to touch him and take away the pain and heal him. He was shocked and amazed that we, Christians, would pray for him, a Muslim.

Though we couldn't stay, we rejoiced that we'd had the opportunity to pray for him.

Ministering in Russia

I went on a short ministry trip to Russia which opened for me an understanding of the Russian people. We saw a lot of fear among the people we met and ministered to. They were hungry for news from the outside and had a very defeated mentality absent of faith in God. We did mostly Bible studies and schools, but we had been warned about a few Christian subjects not to teach. Hopelessness is the best word I can use to describe the places we visited. At one of our gatherings, I ate a few pickles that upset my stomach to the point I could not minister. I stayed in our apartment praying and confessing the Word of God over my hurting stomach. I was not going to a hospital in Russia. Thank God the attack was broken.

27

Back Home Again in Indiana

When the time arrived for us to move back to Anderson, we worked on reestablishing our lives in a fixed location and job. Our church was Full Gospel with a medium-sized congregation that could not support two pastors. We agreed that I would work part-time in the church and find employment outside. I became a local truck driver, which gave me contact with plenty of unchurched people I loved.

It became clear that I had made a mistake in working to get financially wealthy, chasing money and notoriety, which was not the Lord's plan for my life. Helping people was the gift that gave me satisfaction and enjoyment—seeing people come to know the Lord, then finding what gift they had and how to use that gift to glorify the Lord.

We have seen the power of the Holy Spirit to touch and heal in every place the Lord has opened to us. We can say that God is the source of all miracles. He is alive, He is mighty, all-powerful, and ready to help those who need His help, those who will humbly ask for His help and allow Him to get it done in His timing. "For the eyes of the Lord run to and fro throughout the whole earth, to show himself strong on the behalf of them whose heart is perfect toward him" (2 Chronicles 16:9 KJ21).

"Be a facilitator" was the final message from the Lord before we left Brazil. During our last year of living in that country, we met many American mission workers who wanted to visit and work in certain places in Brazil. We helped as many as we could by showing them what we had learned. We discovered that's what a facilitator does, and we were doing that.

Helping others test the mission waters

Upon our return to our local church in Anderson, we asked the Lord to help us locate others to work in foreign missions at various times. These numbered a total of seven husband-and-wife teams plus our middle daughter, Paula.

One of these families moved to Brazil and started a ministry that is still going today and growing. Another pastor has developed a strong connection with a network of churches and has ongoing ministry in two other cities. Another couple joined us for a while and found the right place in Central America. Our daughter Paula taught for five years in a Christian school in Rio. We thank the Lord for these disciples and the work the Lord is doing through them.

This book is about *miracles*. A miracle is a surprising, welcome event that is not explicable by natural or scientific laws and is therefore considered to be the work of a divine agency, an effect or extraordinary event in the physical world that surpasses all known human or natural powers and must be ascribed to a supernatural cause.

We are writing this account to encourage younger believers to listen and hear from God, and if He calls, to answer His call. He

144

is building a Kingdom here on earth, and He needs workers in His harvest—change agents and building blocks.

At some point in your journey, you must decide what you believe and why.
Our culture and our values are shaped by something and someone. My background was a mixture of doctrines and styles of the Bible, music, and what I believed I needed do with my life. I asked myself a few questions on my journey through life: Did I believe there was a God who created heaven and earth? Did I believe the stories written in the Bible were true and why? Was I ready to step out and follow what the Bible reveals?

Take advantage of every opportunity to learn something new and good for helping others.
Why was I raised with two self-taught men who had no education (book wise) to start their own small businesses with no resources? I believe they were modeling that for me, moving forward by faith, trusting in divine providence to succeed.

Do what you can, while you can.
This is what the Lord told me as I was looking at retiring with no good reason to stop. I still had dreams of doing a few things to help the younger generation.

Be a good steward.
Learn how to plan, supervise, manage, and be a trusted, dependable confidant. I taught a class on this in the mission electives. Many of the students confessed they'd never had a class on subjects like these, and they said it benefitted them personally.

Conclusion

This book is an account of how I searched for what was the right thing for me and my family, the right path for me. After my wife and I had our first daughter, I could feel my time and options shrinking in a way I could not understand.

I grew up wanting to be monetarily rich and live a good life, not realizing that I was already rich physically. I had a family around me who loved me and gave me good instructions about life. They kept me on a pathway that was spiritually strong and taught me what was right and good. I pursued my desire to be rich and famous because that was what I wanted to do, not realizing that God had a different plan and purpose for my life. It took some time, a few rocky roads, and many disappointments for me to realize that my desire and my way were not going to work, so I finally let go and let God direct my path. Many other events, not included in this account, were part of our evolving and learning God's guidance on our journey.

My wife and family made this radical change with me, and I am eternally thankful to them for their love and patience as we walked this road together, filled with changes, surprises, and miracles.

About the Authors

When Celester and Cynthia Neeley married over sixty years ago, they had no idea the Lord would call them to the foreign mission field.

In 1970, they moved their three daughters from Chicago's South Side to Anderson, Indiana, and opened up a music business that grew to four stores and a warehouse. Despite their success, they realized that wasn't where they belonged.

Celester's goal was to become a millionaire, but he found himself stressed and confused. The Lord told him if he stayed on that path, he would die. God rebuilt their lives on faith, and they've lived by faith ever since.

In 1984, they traveled to Brazil to represent their local church at Mission Volantes de Cristo near Rio de Janeiro. That grew into twelve years of ministry, living and working alongside their Brazilian brothers and sisters to evangelize the unevangelized areas of Brazil.

From there, they have gone on to experience over forty years of ministry in South America, Europe, Africa, Israel, the US, and other parts of the world.

They now live in Anderson, Indiana. They enjoy their family, which includes three grandchildren.

Celester and Cynthia Neeley's history is one of faith and miracles. They continue to live by faith, and they're quick to say the Lord has never let them down.

They can be contacted at **celestercynthia@gmail.com**.

www.ingramcontent.com/pod-product-compliance
Lightning Source LLC
Chambersburg PA
CBHW071428130425
25066CB00036B/483